PRISONERS OF OUR OWN SUCCESS

FINDING SIGNIFICANCE IN A WORLD MOTIVATED BY SUCCESS

Jason Barr

MORFX PRESS

© 2008 by Jason K. Barr

Published by MORFX Press, a division of Missional Press
149 Golden Plover Drive
Smyrna, DE 19977
www.missional-press.com

Printed in the United States of America

All rights reserved. No part of this publication may be reproduced, stored in a retrieval system, or transmitted in any form or by any means-for example, electronic, photocopy, recording-without the prior written permission of the publisher. The only exception is brief quotations in printed reviews.

Scripture taken from THE HOLY BIBLE, NEW INTERNATIONAL VERSION. Copyright © 1973, 1978, 1984 International Bible Society. Used by permission of Zondervan Bible Publishers.

ISBN-13: 978-0-9798053-5-6
ISBN-10: 0-9798053-5-X

Cover art, concept and design by Sam Raynor.

Table of Contents

Acknowledgements   3

Introduction   5

Chapter 1–What is Success?   11

Chapter 2–How we Perceive Success   33

Chapter 3–What About Fulfillment?   59

Chapter 4–Ladders and Dog Races   83

Chapter 5–What is the True Definition of Success?   107

Chapter 6–Discovering Your Mission   127

Chapter 7–The Brave Few   145

Epilogue   167

About the Author   169

For Sara, Olivia, and Amelia

Success means we go to sleep at night knowing that our talents and abilities were used in a way that served others.

					-Marianne Williamson

Acknowledgements

I don't want to go into a lengthy name-by-name acknowledgement of every person who made this book possible because I would inevitably leave someone out. I do want to thank my wonderful and loving wife, Sara, for always being supportive and encouraging me to follow my passions regardless of how impractical they seem; my beautiful daughters, Olivia and Amelia, for softening me up enough to realize a stick and a rock on a sunny afternoon can be more rewarding than nailing a presentation in a conference room; my extended family for their support, love, and guidance; my pastor, Marty Duren, for his guidance with this book and in my life; and my Savior, Jesus Christ, for helping me realize that it is not all about me.

I am very appreciative to David Phillips at Missional Press for making the whole publishing process much easier for me than I ever thought it would be. Thank you for taking a chance with me. I would also like to thank my editor, Russ

Rankin, for helping untangle my thoughts and make me as coherent as possible.

Last, but certainly not least, I want to thank Sam Raynor for her incredible cover design. She was able to visually capture message of this book and create a cover that I am proud to display. For cover design or other artwork, you may reach her via email, sam@IAMandsam.com.

For more discussion on the topics in this book, please visit my blog at **http://significantblog.wordpress.com**.

Introduction

Our society has more than its share of addictions. You can easily find support groups for people with addictions to drugs, alcohol, gambling, overeating; the list is endless. I wouldn't be surprised if there was a support group for people who are addicted to support groups. I don't mean to belittle those groups; most of them are effective at helping people recover from potentially life-threatening addictions. However, there is another addiction so pervasive in our society that we hardly even recognize it as an addiction. This addiction affects millions of people. It crosses racial, generational, philosophical, and gender barriers. This addiction is seductive to the extent that we often embrace it and emulate those who are most addicted. This is the addiction to success.

Hello, my name is Jason and I am a recovering success addict.

As a young professional experiencing a considerable amount of success in my career, I thought I was on the road to having it all. Promotions came about every other year, bringing with them higher salaries, nicer homes, greater responsibility, and more recognition at higher levels within my company. By the time I was thirty years old, I was the Production Manager in a manufacturing facility that employed more than five hundred people with an annual budget of about seventy-six million dollars. I had the opportunity to give presentations to and rub elbows with high-ranking executives in our company. The future looked bright and I was proud of the work I had done to get to that point.

I had everything mapped out. I would become a plant manager in my mid-thirties and then charge through the ranks at our corporate headquarters. Along the way, I would earn greater responsibility, higher authority, broader recognition, and larger paychecks. At this point in my career, everything was going according to plan. All of the things that society taught me went along with success were coming my way and abundantly so. There was one small problem—I didn't really like what I was doing. In fact, I hated it much of the time.

There were aspects of my job that were rewarding and challenges that kept me engaged. Most of the time, however, I felt that I was ignoring the burning passions for other aspects of my life. Maybe my purpose in life involved more than settling arguments between grown adults, tiptoeing around political hot buttons, and spending three quarters of every day in what seemed to be the same meetings with the same people making the same arguments over the same issues.

Throughout my career, I dealt with the nagging urge to quit my job so that I could spend my life doing something of greater importance. Like many of you, I fantasized about winning the lottery so I could quit my job (which would have been amazing considering that I have never purchased a lottery ticket). If you have never thought of this, go ahead and indulge yourself. Imagine that you just received a windfall of a substantial amount of money. I'm not talking about one of those nine-figure mega-lotteries; just enough money to grant you the financial freedom to do whatever you want for the rest of your life. Think about how differently you would spend your time and what you would do with the money.

Some of you might continue with the same career that you already have because you love it and find a real sense purpose for what you do. If this is you, then this book will be an affirmation of what you already know. Some of you would immediately quit your job so you could go out and blow the money on cars, houses, jewelry, and superfluous luxuries. If you fall into this group, please read on, but understand that you need a lot more help than I can give you. I think the majority of you would fall somewhere in-between. You would give your notice at work, reasonably increase your standard of living, and utilize the time that you once spent on your career to pursue something of greater importance to you.

I believe that the appeal of acquiring a substantial sum of money has less to do with what we could buy with it and more to do with the financial freedom that it would grant. What is financial freedom? I doubt many people reading this are living below or even near the poverty line. You probably don't question where your next meal will come from or if you can afford to pay the electric bill. I think that for most of us, financial freedom means being able to spend our time engaged in activities that are of importance to us without sacrificing the standard of living that we feel we deserve. While that standard of living will fluctuate from person to person, it is grossly bloated for most of us.

Whether you live extravagantly or are a minimalist, you probably feel as if your best chance of acquiring financial freedom is a product of your career and your relative success in it. More success means more money and more money means that you are closer to your notion of financial freedom.

Give some thought to the phrase "financial freedom." If we are seeking freedom, this could only mean that we are prisoners. The resulting paradox is that in our attempts to free ourselves from our prison, we end up fortifying the very walls that imprison us. The only way we can escape is to redefine success.

Consider my situation. Other than a reasonable home mortgage, I was not in debt; my family had all they needed and much of what they desired. For most people, this would constitute financial freedom. What I later came to realize is that I did not feel I had financial freedom because I had given up my time, talents, and passion as collateral in exchange for what others called "success." I didn't have debt in terms of loans or credit cards, but when it came to having the time and energy to pursue anything of real importance, I was deeply in debt.

My goal in writing this book is to offer you my perspective of what constitutes true success so you can think for yourself and decide if you are chasing false success or pursuing true success. I have traveled both paths, so I can offer some insight on the differences between the two. If you fall into the group chasing false success, my further goal is to awaken the passion that once burned within you so you can discover true success.

Do not think of this book as a "How To" guide but more of a "What If" exploration. What if you utilized your time and talents pursuing your passion? What if you cultivated authentic relationships with others in order to influence them and help them rather than using them for your own advancement? What if you decided for yourself what success would look like in your life rather than turning to others to define success for you? What if you stopped being a disciple of false success and discovered your mission?

Chapter 1–What is Success?

When you think of successful people, what attributes come to mind? Do you think of people who love their careers, have balanced lives, and rely on their values to guide them through life's difficult decisions? Do you envision people who may be of modest means, but capitalize on the opportunity to pursue their passions with reckless abandon? Do you conceptualize people who remain low on the corporate ladder so they can maximally utilize their talents? If you are like most in our society, these were probably not your first responses. When we think of successful people, we tend to think of CEOs, doctors, lawyers, high-profile politicians, elite athletes, and entertainers. There are three characteristics generally shared by each of these groups: wealth, power, and recognition. While there is nothing inherently wrong with any of these professions, it is a mistake to use the by-products of success in these fields (money, power, and recognition) to measure our own level of success.

Although material possessions, a wide span of authority, and public notoriety may be tempting, I feel that many of us experience imprisonment from the allure of success itself rather than these fruits of success. We want to feel good about our accomplishments and we want others to respect us for our work. We mistakenly assume that reaching a certain level of societal success will result in a sense of significance and self-worth. We feel that in order to be successful, we have to continually make more money, score higher promotions, and have our names recognized by more people to prove to others that we have indeed made it. This is a distorted view of success and it results in an emptiness we attempt to fill with more success. Because the success we are chasing is false, it will never fill our emptiness and we mistakenly believe that we need to reach even greater levels of success to fill that emptiness. This is not unlike a drug addiction in which higher and higher doses of a drug are required for a user to get high until they finally overdose. In the case of false success, that overdose comes in the form of career burnout, neglecting our families, and losing touch with our priorities in life.

Success is the achievement of something desired. Can we all agree on that? For a CEO, that desire may be gaining market share and increasing profits. For a politician, it may be winning an election for Senate. For an entertainer, it could be landing a feature role in a major motion picture. In any of these fields, achievement will usually result in having more money, more power, and more recognition. Because these are some of the most publicized fields in the media, we view them as the pinnacles of success.

When we watch the news or read a newspaper, we see the multimillion dollar deals made by athletes and entertainers, but not the three percent raise Gary in accounting got last year. We see the homes of those people we deem to be successful decorated with granite countertops in the garage and plasma screen televisions in the bathrooms. We view these niceties as the result of success and have a tendency to use them as benchmarks to measure our success. We do this without even considering what we truly want to achieve—without knowing what would bring us fulfillment and, ultimately, true success.

I am not suggesting that we routinely compare our salary with that of a CEO, our ability to wield power with that of a Washington politician, or our notoriety with that of a Hollywood star in order to determine whether we are successful. I am simply stating that we generally use the categories of money, power, and recognition along with our relative positions in them to identify our level of success. Think about the last time you saw a report on average salaries or household incomes. Didn't you quickly figure out where you were in the spectrum? Once you discovered how your income compared to others, did you let this influence your perception of your success relative to that of others?

Think about how ridiculous that is. You are comparing your level of success, which we earlier defined as the achievement of a desired outcome, to a set of faceless data that simply states how much money people make in a year without even knowing what it is that you or those in the study truly want to achieve. If someone is in the same profession as you and makes fifteen thousand dollars less per year, but they have time to pursue a cause that is more meaningful to them than disposable income, who is more successful?

Money

Let me preface this illustration by stating that this is not an endorsement for the theory of evolution. Nor do I intend for it to give a factual account of the origins of currency. It is just an illustration to get you to think about how we perceive money. Furthermore, lighten up!

The perception of wealth as an indicator of success goes back a long way. Long ago, there was no such thing as money. People were self-sufficient. They would hunt, build, garden, fish, and gather. Money had no value because there was no need to purchase anything. Over time, we became more specialized. People began to discover that they were skilled in specific areas. Consider the following story of Caveman Ted and Neanderthal Ned.

Caveman Ted was a skilled hunter. He could stalk with stealth, track prey, and had the strength to take down the fiercest of animals. Whenever he needed food, he would go to one of his favorite hunting areas and bring home some game. Despite his hunting prowess, Ted was a horrible gardener. He wouldn't have been able to grow corn in Nebraska! Neanderthal Ned, on the other hand, was a gifted gardener. Every year he harvested bushels and bushels of crops. He had learned methods of cultivation that allowed his plants to produce higher yields and always had a better tasting harvest than any of his neighbors.

Ned's problem was that he spent so much time gardening, there was little time left for hunting. Not only that, but because he spent so little time hunting, his hunting skills had diminished to the point that he rarely brought back any game when he did go into the wilderness.

Just when Ned was considering becoming a vegetarian and Ted was on the brink of scurvy, they met up at a prehistoric potluck dinner. Ned brought in his finest crops while Ted contributed his choicest cuts of meat. Other people brought in wonderful items as well. A cave dweller from one of the caves in the Northeast brought what looked like a giant, reddish bug with huge pinchers. He called it "lahbsta." Despite its horrific appearance, Ned and Ted discovered that it was delightful. Another attendee brought in a white liquid that he said he squeezed out of a cow. Apparently, this person spent way too much time in the pasture with nothing else to do. Ned and Ted were quite apprehensive, but it tasted great. It was at this point that Ted discovered he was lactose intolerant, which was a startling revelation shared by all who were near him—caves have notoriously poor ventilation.

After eating their fill, everyone decided that they should get together more often. After a few more dinners, someone suggested setting up a place to trade these newly discovered items so they could enjoy them whenever they wanted. One of the skilled builders offered to build a marketplace in exchange for select items offered in the market. Two days after the completion of the marketplace, the first coffee shop popped up and the mammoth-size half-fat, double-mocha, saber-tooth latte was a huge hit. As people focused more on what they did well, they produced a surplus. This allowed them to trade their excess goods for the items that they desired from the other market participants.

This was a great system. People could focus on what they did well and their society as a whole became more productive. The problem with this system of bartering was that it was not exactly predictable. How many sheepskins was a trained hunting dog worth? If you were a shepherd and your commodity was wool, it would be impossible to know how much wool you would have to produce each year in order to meet the needs of your family. In addition, when people bartered, both of them had to be in the marketplace at the same time. This was a logistical nightmare because cell phone reception in caves is spotty at best.

Finally, someone had the great idea of using a common item of currency to represent the value of each commodity. This would allow a person to sell their item when it was the freshest and in greatest demand, then come back later to buy the items that they needed, when they needed them. Those who could sell more items than they consumed would accrue surplus units of currency. Because it gave them the ability to buy more goods, surplus currency came to represent wealth. Those who were highly skilled at their craft were the ones who grew wealthy. They were capable of producing more of an item than most others could, or they produced a superior product for which people were willing to give up more currency. Either way, wealth directly related to their skills, talents, and success.

In today's culture, we still relate money to success. Therefore, we relate money to skills and talents. The error in this correlation is that the laws of economics must also come into play. Anyone who has ever taken an economics class knows that the principle of supply and demand largely determines market value. This is obvious when dealing with home prices and commodities, but it is also true when we consider the marketability of skills, knowledge, and talents.

For example, you could be the most skilled air conditioner technician in Barrow, Alaska, but you would not make any money without demand for your services. Moreover, because we tend to relate money to success, people would not view you as being successful despite your high level of skill. Now suppose that you enrolled in some training courses and became a furnace technician. Your skill level with furnaces may be just average but because furnace technicians are in high demand in Barrow, Alaska, your marketability increases and you make a lot more money than you did before. By our society's standards, people would consider you more successful even though you perform you job with less skill. You have ceased doing your job with a high level of skill and embraced mainstream adequacy because it pays more and makes other people think that you are more successful.

This is a simplified example, but the same principle applies to many of our professional lives. Several of us resign ourselves to being the furnace technician. Instead of following our passions, we find a job that we know is in demand. We look for the safest, most predictable route that will lead to promotions, raises, and eventual retirement with a nice nest egg. We lie to ourselves by claiming that our career is challenging and our efforts are courageous, but deep down we know that the only reason why we continue in our career is that we are afraid to accept the genuine challenge and show the real courage that it takes to rely on our passion rather than our marketability. We allow the complacency of false success to overrule our longings for fulfillment. We know we can do other things better and we have a burning desire to do them, but they may not supply the surplus currency that we have come to believe defines success.

Remember, we are talking about excess currency; it is not money that imprisons us. We already have all that we really need, but we feel we must have more than we need so others will perceive us as being successful. By settling to do what we feel will lead to success rather than maximizing our talents and pursuing our passions, we are setting ourselves up for a lifetime of internal conflict and a fat, comfortable retirement spent second-guessing our career and life choices.

There is, of course, the other side of this argument that many of us fear. What if we pursue our passions and do not build great wealth? Will we spend our retirement (if we can afford to retire) regretting that we did not go after a more marketable career, and wishing that we had taken the safe route so that we could live more comfortably? While I suppose this is a possibility, I feel we have a deeper desire for fulfillment than we do for a gargantuan 401(k). Almost any fool can make money and amass huge sums of it over time. If you don't believe me, just look at the people who have accomplished this very thing. It is much rarer to find a person who authentically loves what they do than to find one who makes substantial sums of money doing it.

Power

Power is also associated with success and achievement. When we were children, superheroes fascinated us because of their superhuman strength and abilities. Young boys flex their muscles and attempt to show that they are more powerful than their adversaries. Young girls are attracted to the boys with the greatest display of power (or at least that is what the boys believe). Precisely the same theme is present in nature. Rams beat their heads together, deer use their racks to battle each other, peacocks strut with their finest plumage extended, and humans establish organizational charts.

You may think that we are more civilized than our zoological counterparts, but once the organizational charts are established, we beat our heads, battle each other and extend our plumage to get to the top of the heap. We do this in an attempt to display our dominance and establish our position in the hierarchy of our society. To us, the amount of power that we have amassed comes to represent the validation of others, which is the basis of self-esteem for many. When we acquire more power, we feel that people have witnessed our performance and regarded it more highly than the efforts of others. We believe that power has a direct linkage to our success.

It is generally true that as we become more successful, we will accumulate more authority. There is nothing wrong with this formula as long as we obtain authority in the areas in which we are talented. We begin to go astray when we equate authority with power and the need to display it. In the business world, we associate power with how high a person is on the organizational chart. The more squares you have under you, the more powerful you are. It is even better if the squares under you have squares under them. You do not have to be in a multilayered corporation for this concept to hold true. If you are a sole proprietor, you will become more powerful in your relationship with customers and suppliers as you become more successful.

Power in itself is not bad—we just have to respect it and not make the quest for more power the driving ambition of our careers. In the business world, the linkage of success to positional power leads us into a never-ending effort to gain more power by climbing higher up the ladder. We feel that in order to capitalize on the success we have already achieved and influence a group, we must be the head of that group. After we spend some time as the head of that group, we feel that we need to become the head of the department in which that group falls. Then we must become the head of the facility, district, region, and so forth. Our corporate culture teaches us that if we fail to move to that next level, we are unsuccessful and lack ambition. In doing so, we have mistakenly equated contentment with complacency.

In many instances, striving to make it to the next level is a legitimate goal, but far too often, we do so at the expense of where we are today. As we remain focused on where we are going, we can also forget from where we came. We forget about relationships, we ignore consequences and we may even fall into the epitome of the improper use of power: the power struggle.

We have all witnessed power struggles. They can be at work, in a family situation, at church, in a political environment, or in a civic organization. Wherever three or more people are involved, there is the potential for a power struggle. I believe the magic number of people required for an organizational power struggle is three because although two people can have a conflict, a real display of power is only necessary when there is an audience. Peacocks have little reason go about strutting when there is no one to admire their plumage.

Probably the most common arena for public displays of power is at work. More often than not, the person displaying the power has some serious self-esteem issues. I am not talking about aggressive leaders who know how to get the most out of their employees. I am talking about those people who are so insecure about their abilities and how others will perceive them that their only defense is to try to make other people look bad in hopes that they will look good by comparison. They ruin reputations, inflict collateral damage on innocent bystanders, and destroy relationships all for the sake of showing how powerful they are. How can this be an indicator of success?

It is incredibly frustrating to witness people who don't consider the big picture as they position their chess pieces in an effort to make themselves look better. Some even instigate conflict just so they can demonstrate their power. They are like children in the schoolyard trying to impress their peers.

It is ironic that by definition, the word corporate means to be united and combined in one body. But the more "corporate" a business is, the more these internal power struggles tend to arise and the less united that business becomes. This was probably the biggest driving factor in my decision to leave the corporate world. People were more concerned with the perception of their success than they were with the reality of their problems.

So does power come with success? To some extent, the answer is "yes." When abused, however, power leads to failure. Think about some of the most effective leaders that you know. Most likely, they do not rule with a heavy hand and a lengthy list of mandates. In my experience, the most successful leaders are those who challenge you to *want* to do your best all the time. Sure, a strict, legalistic boss can keep people in line while watching over them, but what happens when the boss is away? The people usually revert to their old ways only to snap back into form when the boss comes around. That boss may think that he has a great deal of power because when he says jump, people jump—he sees it with his own eyes. This, however, is not power, but intimidation. True power is being able to influence a person's decisions without even being physically present. Leading people according to values, not rules, and with a helping hand rather than a firm fist can best accomplish that task.

Humility, not a display power, is the trademark of a truly successful person. Humility allows a leader to admit they may be wrong and to seek alternative strategies. Whenever leaders make themselves vulnerable by admitting they do not know everything and that they need the people they lead to help steer the ship, they gain credibility and buy-in from those they lead. None of us is infallible and we all know it. To pretend to be so only makes apparent our lack of self-esteem and maturity. If we pretend that we have all the answers and never make mistakes, the people we lead and manage will see right through our false visage and we will instantly lose their respect. So why don't we exhibit more humility? Once again, I think the answer lies in the illusion of false success.

Those driven by power would shy away from putting themselves in a vulnerable position because they believe that any admission of error is a sign of weakness and any sign of weakness may be an opening for their adversaries to diminish their power. Their need to cling to power is actually one of the most telling signs of their weakness. It is this "I am smarter than you, harder working than you, and better than you" mentality that isolates them from others and severely limits their ability to connect with people and develop relationships, which are key components to true success.

Don't think you can get off the hook here just because you outwardly display humility. While outward humility will help you gain the respect of those you lead, we need to be careful to avoid false humility when it comes to power. For many of us, simply having power for the sake of being powerful is not a driving factor in our lives. We do, however, enjoy the feeling that we are worthy of having power bestowed upon us. This can result in a conflict between what we want to do with our lives and how we want others to perceive us. If we allow ourselves to become enamored with the concept of success and fall into the false belief that the amassing of power relates directly to success, we will begin to head down a road that will indeed bring us more power, but it will also likely take us away from our passions, our mission, and true success.

Those who fit the description of false humility may feel that they are humble because they are not compelled to flex their organizational chart muscles or constantly berate their employees. Because power does not motivate them, they may feel that their humility is genuine. They 'fess up to their mistakes, give credit where credit is due, and may even use self-depreciating humor. All of these characteristics do indeed give the outward appearance of humility. Ask these people to step down from their current level of authority; however, and you will find that their power is very dear to them. Challenge their humility and they will defend it. Think about that for a moment.

If a person feels the need to defend their humility, that is actually an expression of pride—the exact opposite of humility.

I know this group well because I struggled with this issue for many years. I wanted to get out of my corporate job and pursue something more in line with my passions, but I found that giving up the level of responsibility and authority I had reached in my professional life was even more difficult than giving up the paychecks that came with them. I wasn't power-hungry, but I was success-hungry, and in my mind, I believed that if I stepped away from the level of power I had obtained, then people would no longer view me as being successful. Frankly, this scared the daylights out of me. Many of you are probably the same way. Outwardly, you appear to be humble—and inwardly you may even believe this to be true—but if you are investing in your career primarily because of the status that you believe it gives you in the eyes of others, humility has lost and pride has taken over.

Alternatively, there may be a noble reason for gaining power and authority, such as using it to do good things and help others. Some people really do fall into this category, and that is great as long as it is the truth. However, if you say that helping others is your driving goal, I have a feeling that other avenues would better facilitate reaching that goal—many of which you may not even consider because they would require you to relinquish your current level of power and authority. Eventually, the ulterior motive of achieving an outward appearance of success will erode your mission and prevent you from attaining true success.

Recognition

The third component our culture uses to measure success is recognition. To most of us, recognition means being able to pick out a face in a crowd. In a large company, we may measure recognition by the number of people in other facilities and offices that recognize our work or us. A common tactic for the achievement of corporate recognition is for someone to have that one shining success story on which to stamp their name.

If you have worked in an environment where the big bosses come in for visits, you have seen this play out many times. Different companies have different cultures, but the scenario usually goes something like this:

A high-level executive or director from the corporate office comes to visit your facility and check up on how things are operating. During a tour of the office/facility, your boss introduces you to the newest director.

Your boss smiles at you, turns to the new director, and says, "Mr. Pleated Khaki, I'd like you to meet Ima Realperson."

As Mr. Khaki shakes your hand, you can tell that he is searching the "shining moment" database in his head to uncover a project with which he can associate your name. In a matter of seconds, he replies, "Oh yes, you're the one who developed the new documentation system that tracks changes to our documentation system that controls the approval system that allows changes to documents."

You glow inside with the knowledge that you have been recognized for your work and go on to tell Mr. Khaki far more

25

than he ever wanted to know about your project. You are proud of the fact that you obtained recognition for what you have done, but you overlook the fact that your work has not had a lasting positive impact on another person. In fact, while developing your system, you probably actually gave more consideration to how the system would look to those from above, rather than how it would work for those that actually use it—those with whom you have the greatest opportunity to leave a positive and lasting impact.

When your review time rolls around, your boss highlights this project in your appraisal with no mention of the countless decisions you made, relationships you mended, fires you extinguished, or problems you circumvented every other day of the year. Your review completely ignores the many relationships that you cultivated in order keep operations running smoothly and focuses on the documentation system and other tangible projects on which you worked, whether completed or not, because they are easy to define, measure, and track.

If you have ever been in this situation, think about what made you proud. Was it the actual culmination of your efforts into a working system or was it simply the recognition? There are some instances where the former is true but this is rare. Because we undertake many of our endeavors in search of short-term success and the proverbial "feather in our cap," the feeling of success does not usually come as a product of our efforts but from the recognition of them.

What will be the eventual fate of the actual system you developed? Will it be effective a year from now? Chances are it won't because you will move on and your successor will reinvent the wheel in order to obtain his or her own feather. Furthermore, will it even bother you that the system you worked so hard to establish is no longer in effect? Not if it was not the system itself, but the recognition for creating it that motivated you. Besides, by the time your successor comes along to erase your efforts, you will be busy erasing those of your predecessor. Eventually, this becomes an endless cycle of individuals performing work for the sake of recognition and not out of a passion for what they do. As this cycle repeats itself, we reinforce the concept that the recognition of our work leads to success, until we finally learn to become numb to our passions because they do not fit neatly into our picture of success.

Earlier, we discussed humility and its role as a key element to sound leadership and true success. This is in stark contrast to what the business world teaches us. I am not implying that companies are in the habit of putting on three-day workshops focusing on the evils of humility—the formal training that you receive from your employer would probably tell you that humility is a good thing. The problem with formal training is that the muffins and cookies served at break time usually stick with us longer than the training we receive from those seminars and workshops. The lasting lessons we learn from the business world are those taught to us every day as we observe the cause and effect relationships between a coworker's actions and their resulting fate. I have witnessed exceptionally gifted leaders—because of their humility—not receive promotions they deserve. At the same time, I have seen horrendous leaders continue to move up the ladder—not because of what they have done—but because of how much attention they draw to themselves. What are we to learn from this lesson? I think I can summarize it by stating that in today's corporate culture, what we do is not as important as the recognition we can draw to ourselves while we are doing it.

On the surface, this is dangerous because it results in countless unfinished projects, systems that do not work on a long-term basis, and the advancement of employees unworthy of their promotions. On a deeper level, it causes damage to the psyche of the employee. This mentality causes us to no longer utilize our talents and pursue our passions, but instead to chase the latest whim of those above us in hopes that our efforts will grant us the recognition we feel is necessary make us successful. The result is a workforce made up of uninspired people who do not even know their potential for true success. If they would just surrender to their own personal mission and stop trying to look successful to others in society, they may actually discover true success.

While false success does result in some degree of short-term recognition, that recognition is fleeting. True success, on the other hand, will result in a legacy. If you have studied leadership very much, you understand the importance of this concept. I think we have a tendency to oversimplify what it means to leave a legacy. A legacy is not a system that other people manage after you move on. It is not a collection of fairy tales about your exploits. It is not having your image enshrined on the wall of the office lobby. I believe that to leave a legacy is to cause a fundamental change in the thought process and culture of a group.

We will talk more about this later, but for now, it is important that we differentiate between doing work for the reward or recognition that we will receive from others and doing work because of the reward it produces by fulfilling our mission and because we were meant to do it. If the accolades and recognition you receive from others motivates you, but your work is not meaningful to you, then you can never be truly successful. You will only achieve true success when you align your work with your mission and your mission with your values.

Have you ever heard anyone make the statement that they want to "be somebody"? When people say this, they are usually expressing their desire to do something to gain recognition on a broad scale. They want to put their mark on the world and gain recognition for their efforts. We believe that if the masses will recognize our work, then we will be successful. But ask yourself the following question: Of all the people who have had the greatest impact in your life, how many are widely recognized? Conversely, of all the people who are widely recognized, how many have been truly influential to you? If you really put some thought into this, I believe you will find that some of the greatest opportunities for success are in your own backyard.

If we are to seek true success, then our goal should be to become people of influence, not recognition. We need to focus on how we affect others rather than how we can gain their praise. Some of you are in a position or a career that gives you numerous opportunities every day to have a lasting positive impact on others. Others of you may struggle with how to incorporate this touchy-feely stuff into your day-to-day activities. If you fall into the latter group, you have a couple of options. The most drastic (though possibly necessary) option would be to make a career change if you feel you are unable to fulfill your mission while pursuing your current career. Another option is simply to change your mindset and to cease defining your entire life by what you do to earn a living.

Your career is a very big part of your life and you dedicate much of your time and energy to it. However, if you allow your job title to dictate what you can or cannot do in the lives of others, you are setting yourself up for an ongoing struggle between the person you **portray** at work everyday and the person that you desire to be. **While** the person that you portray may be able to attain **recognition**, thereby creating success as defined by others, it **could be at** the expense of your true self by ignoring what you **most desire**. Remember that the definition of success is the achie**vement of** something desired, so if you focus your efforts on recognition **without** considering your desires, you will never become **truly successful**.

Thinking for Yourself

The purpose of this book is not to give you a systematic process by which you will attain true success. My only goal is to get you to think. I want you to stop blindly following a career path of mundane external success like a lemming marching over the edge of a cliff. I want you to search yourself and discover your purpose instead of focusing on what will bring you a predictable level of "success." I want you to stop letting others determine where you focus your efforts based on how they perceive your talents and instead focus on how you can positively utilize them.

There is a very good chance that you feel the same way, or you would not be reading this book. You have probably had a taste of false success and while it may have been temporarily delicious, you found that it was not sustaining. Just like the foods that we consume, those that offer the most nutrition are rarely the ones that we consider the tastiest while we are eating them. If we were to base our diet solely on taste, we would eventually suffer the consequences of poor health. Likewise, what we may falsely define as success is sometimes nothing more than the professional equivalent of junk food. It tastes good initially, but leaves us with indigestion, heartburn, and obesity.

I challenge you to consider what motivates you. Even if it is not the outward appearance of success, does the inner desire to be successful imprison you? Will you risk becoming a failure in the eyes of others in order to follow your passions? Can you extend the arena of success beyond your career to include all aspects of your life? These are critical questions to ask yourself as you move toward true success.

Chapter 2–How we Perceive Success

In the preceding chapter, we saw how society defines success. At this point, you may be thinking that you are different and society's definition of success doesn't really apply to you. While money, power, and recognition may not be your sole motivators, I am willing to bet that those attributes do factor in to your assessment of your overall level of success. Even if it is only on the subconscious level, I think we have a tendency to compare what we have with what others have.

I have struggled in this area. I found myself wanting certain material possessions not for the luxury or utility that they offered, but because of the visual level of success that I believed they represented. I was afraid that if others owned houses or cars superior to mine, they would not regard my level of success as being on par with theirs. I made it a competition with no real winner. I know this sounds immature and weak-minded, but if you look around you'll find that this thought process is pervasive in our society.

Beyond the materialistic level, we may attempt to validate our success according to what others think of us. This is where we truly become prisoners of our success. We focus so much on achieving success—as defined by others—that we lose sight of our own goals. The obvious dilemma here is that if we cannot see our own goals, we can never really be successful. The resulting paradox is that we never achieve true success in our personal lives or even know what constitutes true success because we are reduced to seeking a false sense of success that is defined by others. It seems that we are more concerned with proving ourselves to others than we are with seeking out and fulfilling our personal mission.

I believe that if we make the effort to understand our mission and pursue our passions, then we will be much less concerned about what others think about us and whether or not they view us as being "successful." Unfortunately, most of us don't have a clue what our mission is or we are too afraid to pursue it. As a result, we cannot measure our lives in terms of true success. We lack the authentic sense of success that comes from achieving that which we most desire and the fulfillment of knowing that we are acting in a capacity that maximizes our skills and talents. Having lost or never known the fulfillment of true success, we turn to those indicators of success that we can easily measure, universally communicate, and prominently display.

Checking In with the Joneses

The fact that you are reading this book indicates that you have probably experienced a fair amount of growth in your career and are likely in some sort of leadership position. Because of this, you are inclined to have a competitive streak in you. Competition is good. It is the fundamental principle of capitalism. Without competition we would see inflated prices, little technological advancement, and I wouldn't be able to watch college football for twelve straight hours on Saturdays in the fall.

But what happens when competition spills over into our personal lives? We are no longer dealing with the competition to *do* something better, but the competition to *have* something better. While we could use the term "ambition" to describe the competition to *do* something, we could describe the competition to *have* something as "greed." By today's standards, most of you probably don't consider yourself as greedy. However, today's skewed standards make it difficult to recognize greed anymore.

Think about the average home. According to the National Association of Home Builders, the average size of a newly constructed American home in 1978 was 1,750 square feet. By 2006, that number had swelled to 2,456 square feet.[1] This is a 40 percent increase in the size of new homes over a period in which the average number of people living in those homes actually went down.

The expansion of the American home did not happen overnight. In fact, the average home size only increased about 1

---

[1] "Single Family Square Footage by Location." 25 July 2007 <www.nahb.org/fileUpload_details.aspx?contentID=80051> Source: U.S. Census Bureau

to 2 percent from one year to the next. As our friends, families, and people on television that we don't even know moved into newer and bigger homes, we felt the desire and pressure to have more. We did not have to outdo them by much, but just enough to show that we could do it. That gradual process of "one-upping" can result in significant long-term changes. I say this not to condemn anyone living in a large home, but to illustrate how small, almost unnoticeable changes can lead to drastic changes over time.

The numbers speak for themselves. We all know what compound interest can do for a 401(k) and the preceding illustration shows how compounding home sizes can result in tremendous shifts over several years, but what about compounding greed? I am not aware of a "greed index," but if one existed, I am quite certain that we would see exponential growth as our society has and desires more. You can see greed growing from generation to generation. Right now, we have a lot more "stuff" than any of our ancestors. Yet we also seem to be more discontent with what we have. What does that tell us? If we have more "stuff" and are less content, we can conclude that more "stuff" will not make us happy! The fleeting joy of having the newest, biggest, and best gadget is what makes us feel good. The problem with this is that it is a superficial happiness and it lasts only until a newer and better gadget comes out.

The past three vehicles I have owned have all been a particular make and model of the same pickup truck. The last two I bought were fully loaded—leather interior, upgraded stereo system, heated seats and mirrors (because it is very important to have heated seats and mirrors when you live in Georgia), and several other features that I don't even know how to use. If the manufacturer offered it as an option, I had it. I remember how proud I was of those new vehicles and how I imagined other people envying me as I drove down the road. With these last two vehicles, however, I fell off my perch at the pinnacle of pickup truck smugness when the manufacturer came out with a completely new body style shortly after I bought my new vehicles. How disappointing is it to buy a brand new vehicle only to see the manufacturer come out with a new body style the next year? How much more disappointing is it when the guy three houses down from you buys the newest body style and completely makes you obsolete in the rankings of the Joneses?

Whether we want to admit it or not, it is human nature to compare what we have to what others have. The theme of greed goes all the way back to the Biblical story of Adam and Eve. Those two had it pretty good. They had the opportunity to frolic around in the Garden of Eden with no worries and no stress. They didn't have to worry about traffic, environmental concerns, health issues, or the latest fashion trends. All they had to do was enjoy the garden and stay away from that one forbidden fruit. This should have been an easy task to manage when you consider that they could have anything else in the garden and were the only two humans on the earth at the time. They didn't have neighbors growing a seductive forbidden fruit patch, nor were they bombarded with forbidden fruit commercials on television. But they still gave in to temptation.

What was it that caused them to surrender to temptation? The serpent told Eve that if they ate the fruit, they would gain the knowledge of good and evil and be like God. Up to this point, it does not appear that Eve had any interest in the fruit until she learned that God had something that she didn't have and that the way to get it was by eating the fruit. Her response to this desire to have something else—even though she lacked nothing—led to the Fall of Man. She and Adam ate fruit, which resulted in their banishment from the garden, painful childbirth, difficulties with work, and people driving slowly in the left lane.

In a sense, the Fall of Man all boils down to Adam and Eve's temptation and desire to keep up with the Joneses. In their case there were no Joneses, so they became envious of God Himself. You can metaphorically relate the serpent to a commercial telling them that there was something else out there that would make them happy—something that they didn't even know they wanted. Just like us with all of our objects of desire, they didn't need the fruit, but they were tempted by a third party who pointed out that they lacked something.

In Adam and Eve's case, giving in to temptation led to their separation from God and introduced the concept of sin. The degree to which we allow greed and pride to corrupt our lives varies by individual, but it can be terribly destructive. If we allow the various serpents in our world to tempt us into striving to have objects of desire rather than pursuing our passions, we are committing an evil on par with Adam and Eve eating the forbidden fruit.

You may be thinking, "How can my pursuit of success be equated to the original sin?" The answer is quite simple. The New Testament tells us that sin is not limited to doing bad things. It tells us that if we know we should do something and don't do it, that is sin.[2] It also tells us that anything that separates us from God and His will is sin. This could be the original sin committed by Adam and Eve or the sin of omission that we commit by not

---

[2] John 15:1-4, James 4:17

using our gifts to pursue our given mission. It all comes down to greed, pride, and our malcontent with what we *have* because deep down we know that there is something lacking in what we *do*.

While greed is nothing new, our society enhances it. Many other societies believe that money motivates the people of the United States. While money has a significant impact on what we do, the places we go, and the things we possess, I am of the opinion that entertainment is a greater controlling factor in our society. Financial advisors excluded, people usually don't stand around the water cooler talking about whether or not the Fed increased interest rates. They talk about the latest reality television show or a sporting event they watched last night. What else happens while we are entertained? We see a multitude of commercials. The typical commercial goes like this: You are not happy with what you have... This is our product... People who have this product are happy... If you buy this product, you will be happy. Does that sound familiar? Before long, you fill your home with things that you never use or even want, simply because at one time you thought a particular item would somehow make you happier than you were before you owned it.

Another way that entertainment fuels our desire to have more is that it vastly increases the base from which we can compare what we have to what others have. Not very long ago, the only way people could compare themselves with the Joneses was by seeing firsthand what the Joneses had. Now there are millions of Joneses no further away than our television set or the Internet. This lays a foundation for greed on a much broader scale than experienced by any of our ancestors. This broader base of comparison causes us to become more extravagant in our desires and less satisfied with what we already have.

Why has entertainment become such a force in our lives? Why do we waste countless hours staring at a television set? Why do we spend nearly twice the minimum wage on a single movie ticket? It is because our lives lack adventure and the pursuit of what we really want to achieve. We have extinguished the flame of what was once a burning passion within us. When we were children, every day was an adventure. Matchsticks in a ditch became infantrymen from the opposing forces that were coming up the ravine to attack. The only hope for your troop's survival was your sniper skills and a trusty pellet rifle. Your pet Labrador was a ferocious, wild animal that only you could tame to protect your friends. A pile of cardboard boxes was an impenetrable fortress where you could seek refuge from dragons and trolls.

Somewhere along the journey to adulthood, our sense of adventure vanished. Unquestionably, our lives still have moments of crisis and drama, but this is generally something that we view as unwanted and not in accordance to our carefully laid plans. We believe that with maturity comes the responsibility to plan every aspect of our lives and to do so in a manner that involves the least amount of risk. This means taking the job that will provide financial security, good insurance, and a retirement package. This job may also deaden our souls and repress our desires, but we believe that to be the price we must pay for safe, secure, and predictable success. This approach is both arrogant and boring.

Because of the self-inflicted boredom that results from censuring our passions, we turn to the artificial world of entertainment for any sense of adventure, romance, or acts heroism—the very things that make up a life of pursuing our passions and fulfilling our personal mission. Sure, the consequences are greater in real life and there are no soundtracks to get you pumped up when you need a shot of adrenaline or to warn you of imminent danger, but our lives can be much greater stories than those that we see in the movies. Don't you think that we have it backwards if we resign our daily lives to boredom and predictability only to turn to the artificial world of entertainment get our action and adventure fix?

What Will People Think of Me?

During my career in the corporate world, I felt trapped. I knew that I lacked passion for most of the aspects my job, but I was afraid that people would think less of me if I did something other than utilize my engineering degree and management experience. I daydreamed about how refreshing it would be to do something more fulfilling, and I know I was not alone in this feeling because many others with whom I confided felt the same way. Despite their widespread discontent, many of those people never got out of their prison cells because they were afraid of what others would think.

Early in my career, my entrapment was due largely to the financial security of my job. I was doing well and the road ahead looked even better—a common snare for many young professionals. As I moved into roles of greater responsibility, the financial security continued to grow but that was not what bound me to my career. I felt that if I turned away from the success I had achieved, people would think less of me. I worried that people who knew me and knew about my success would think of me as a quitter if did not continue down the road I had started.

I was also concerned about what would happen when I met new people. Whenever we meet a person for the first time, inevitably someone asks, "So, what do you do?" Even though I was not happy with what I did for a living, I felt a sense of pride when given the opportunity to explain it to someone who had never met me. I was afraid that people would not think as highly of me if I did not have the opportunity to enlighten them with the immense responsibility, leadership, and stress that my job entailed (this is written sarcastically). I finally realized that most people didn't care what I did and those who did care were likely ego-driven narcissists who stopped listening to me halfway through my soliloquy to devise a description of their job that would trump mine.

That's when it hit me. If people who linked job titles and careers to a person's self-worth were ego-driven narcissists and I felt that I had to have a certain career path so others would think highly of me, it only follows that I was an ego-driven narcissist. I finally came to realize that I was not afraid of what others would think of me, I was afraid of what I would think of myself. I thought that if I did not spend my time and energy striving for ever-increasing levels of success, I would be wasting my talents and education.

If you find yourself in this situation, I have a simple cure. Imagine that you are limited to accomplishing five things before you die. Take some time to write down what those five things would be. For most people, your list will consist of items that deal with relationships—your relationship with your family and friends, your relationship with God, your relationship with yourself, and your relationship with society.

Once you are satisfied with your list, think about how you would achieve each item. Next to each item on your list, write a statement about how you can have a positive influence in each of those areas that will still be effective fifty years from today. Finally, write down what you need to do on a daily basis to bring about that lasting influence.

Now take some time to consider what you are currently doing in your daily routine. It is very probable that the things you do everyday have absolutely nothing to do with what is of the most importance to you. My counsel is not to worry about what other people think about you. Take the time and effort for some honest introspection and figure out what you really think about yourself. Discover what is of most importance to you, set goals that will have lasting effects in those areas, and align your daily efforts with achieving those goals. If you do these things, you will quickly realize how ridiculous your everyday life was before. Your self-esteem will reach a level that no ego-driven narcissist will ever be able to shake.

Where Does Guilt Come Into Play?

When I discuss the concept of a person's success binding them to a certain job or career, another common theme arises. People feel as though the welfare of others relies on them continuing to perform their job. This typically manifests itself in two ways. The people you support financially rely on you for income and security, while the people you work with rely on you to improve their workplace. In both of these situations, we are talking about providing for the needs of others.

In various areas throughout this book, I discuss the importance of seeking ways to positively affect others in our careers. Obviously, providing for our families and improving our workplace has a positive impact that benefits others. However, just as we have allowed the definition of success to become shallow and external, we have done the same with the concept of providing for our families and improving the condition of our workplace. We dumb it down to the superficial level of making people happy for the moment without considering their long-term needs. As we are about to see, we often sacrifice the long-term needs of our families and coworkers for the sake of instant gratification.

Providing for Our Families

This is one of the most common excuses people use for not pursuing their passions. People say that they want their children to have a better life than they had growing up or that they want their families to live "the good life." More often than not, what we call providing for our families is actually competitive materialism. We hear our children talk about the new car that Bobby's dad just purchased or the house that Sally's family recently moved into and our internal reaction is that we are somehow losing a materialistic competition. We feel that we are letting our children and our families down because we failed to match the materialistic excess enjoyed by each of their friends.

I think we need to take some time to investigate what it means to provide for our families. Back in Caveman Ted and Neanderthal Ned's day, that meant providing food, shelter, and security. Today, we feel that providing for our families requires expensive vacations, college and possibly even private school tuition, expensive video games, a nice home with all the amenities enjoyed by the families to which we compare our level of success, and a new car for our children by the time they turn sixteen. We concentrate so much on "providing" for our families that we fail to realize their actual needs. In doing so, we are failing them.

This is a good time to look at Maslow's hierarchy of needs. Abraham Maslow was an American psychologist who studied the motivation of some exceptional people. If you have ever taken a management or psychology course, you have probably seen the five-layer pyramid used to illustrate his theory of the hierarchy of human needs. We are going to look at the foundation of this pyramid.

At the base of the pyramid are the needs we have as living organisms—food, water, oxygen, and basic bodily functions. The next level up consists of our security needs. Security does not just refer to protection from grizzly bears and sub-prime mortgages. It also pertains to the security of employment, financial security, security in our health, security of the family unit, and security in our morals. In our society, we seem to concentrate on financial security at the expense of security of the family unit and morals.

What does it mean to have security in the family unit? Think about the example you set for your children by the way you interact with your spouse and other family members. If there is any marital tension between you and your spouse, your children will sense it. In fact, many behavioral problems with children are not as much a result of the child's personality or your parenting skills as they are a result of your relationship with your spouse. If you disagree with this statement, I encourage you to do some research on the subject. For now, I think it is sufficient to say that children who are secure in Mom and Dad's relationship stand a better chance of realizing family security than children who constantly question whether their family will stay intact.[3]

This is where a lot of us steer off course. Because we are focusing more on providing for our families financially and materialistically, we are enduring higher stress levels and working longer hours that result in the degradation of our marriages and family life. We mean well; we are just placing our efforts in the wrong area. Think about how much time and energy you are currently pouring into providing financial security for your family and compare that to how much time and energy you are dedicating to providing your family security in itself. It may be time to reevaluate your family's true needs and adjust your lifestyle accordingly.

As successful professionals, many of you probably have more money than time. Since it is scarcer, you value your time more highly than your money. You can fool yourself into

---

[3] For more information on this subject, I encourage you to read Gary Ezzo and Robert Bucknam, *On Becoming Baby Wise* (Louisiana, Missouri: Parent-Wise Solutions a division of Charleston Publishing Group Incorporated, 2001, orig. 1995)

believing that you are being generous because you buy your family gifts or send money to a charitable cause, but in reality you are giving a resource that you value less (money) so that you can dedicate the more valuable one (time) to the prideful pursuit of success and self-advancement. When it comes to the needs of your family, the excessive financial security that your money can provide does not even come close to the basic family security your time can provide. We talk about a life/work balance and say that our family is more important, only to put in sixty- to seventy-hour workweeks. Add in the time we spend commuting to our jobs and working from home and we are fortunate if we end up with two or three hours a day for our families. Those precious few hours that we do have with them are riddled with stress over our jobs, causing us to be present in body but absent in mind and spirit. It seems that if we cannot fill our family's needs with our presence, then we try to do so with presents.

Another need that we apparently have some trouble with is the security of our morals. In the same manner that corporate seminars and workshops often oppose corporate culture, if we are telling our children one thing and living differently, we are sending a mixed signal. Almost without exception, it is the morals we teach through our actions and not our words that we reinforce. For example, let's say you take your kids shopping. One of them sees a particularly tasty looking treat at the checkout line and expresses their desire to have it. Since you are on your way home to have dinner, you tell them that they cannot have the treat and a tantrum ensues.

The problem is not their desire to have the treat, but their reaction to you denying them what they want. Eventually, you calm the child down and tell them not to throw a tantrum or lose their temper. On your way home, you explain to them that tantrums are childish and show a lack of self-control. As you are making this glorious Heathcliff Huxtable speech from your memories of *The Cosby Show*, someone cuts you off in traffic and you react with your own tantrum and loss of temper. What message are you sending? I live near Atlanta, so this is a very tough one for me. Just remember that the lessons that we reinforce with our families come from what we do, more often than from what we say.

This is a simplified example in which the disagreement between the morals we teach and those by which we live is obvious. There are many other contradictions if we pay closer attention and realize that children are not only learning morals while watching a wholesome television special or at church, but also by the everyday experiences you encounter as a parent and how you handle them. We tell our children not to talk badly about their fellow classmates and then we go on a rant about a "stupid" coworker whose opinions do not happen to be identical to ours. We tell our children they should share, yet we fail to capitalize on opportunities to demonstrate generosity through charitable giving and service to others. We tell our children they cannot have every toy they see and that they should be happy with what they already have, only to obsess over a home, a car or a job that we mistakenly assume will bring us happiness. We tell our families that they are our top priority and then we pour the majority of our time and energy into our careers under the false pretense that we are doing it for the good of our families. I think you get the picture.

All of these inconsistencies lead to moral confusion. Since they are not getting consistent moral direction from their parents, children may turn elsewhere for clarification. Some may go to friends; some go to teachers, but an overwhelming number turn to television and other forms of entertainment. They see people on television who deal with similar problems and follow the lead of fictitious characters created for the generation of advertising revenue instead of turning to the values and morals that you need to instill as a parent. This is what it means to have a lack of security in our morals. It is not the media's fault, the teacher's fault, or the friend's fault. It is our fault because we failed as parents by making the pursuit of success and the provision of excessive materialistic items a higher priority than providing sound moral guidance and offering leadership to the people who mean the most to us.

The third level up the pyramid involves social needs. This is our need for belonging to a group and the need to be loved by others. As humans, we have a natural desire for acceptance by groups of people. This is true at work, in the classroom, on the playground, and especially at home. Our children need to know that they are part of something bigger; they are part of a family. Each family needs to have an identity complete with traditions, morals and expectations. Each member of the family needs to understand that their actions not only reflect on them as individuals, but on the family as well. This is a great responsibility and we should not take it lightly.

In many homes, it is "every man for himself." Parents have little time to spend with their children because of their busy work schedule. The time that they do spend with their children seems rushed and filled with stress leftover from the workday. The home lacks a social family entity to which children can belong; therefore, they seek to belong elsewhere. Some turn to sports, religious groups, or special interest clubs, while others may turn to gangs, drugs, or sexual predators for their sense of belonging. The effect of turning to groups outside the family for a sense of belonging can be harmless or it can be devastating.

The responsibility of every parent is to ensure that a family social structure exists. The best way to do this is by spending time with your family nurturing this dynamic social structure. How much time this requires depends on your family and each member's needs. For some of you, it may require more time away from your job. Many of us refuse to accept this reality. We tell ourselves that we have responsibilities at work that we cannot let slide and deadlines we must meet or else we will lose our job. Do you honestly believe that your responsibilities to your job are greater than your responsibilities to your family?

You may say it is because of your responsibility to your family that you must put in the long hours and come home overworked, overstressed, and disconnected. You think it is a badge of honor to persevere through these hardships so your family will be financially secure. I say that this is an outright lie and every one of us knows it!

We put in the extra hours and effort because we are in the never-ending quest for more success. We know we could work a reasonable number of hours, have time to spend with our families, and still provide for their financial needs—perhaps not as lavishly as we could if we kept chasing that brass ring, but we can provide for them nonetheless. "But I want my family to have the very best," you say. I ask you—the best of what? If you want them to have the best clothes, the best cars, the best stainless steel appliances, and the best plasma screen televisions, then by all means continue to allow your desire for a bigger paycheck preclude their desire to belong to a family unit. However, your family does not want the best of those things – they want the best of you. Many of us give our best to careers and the pursuit of success only to offer a few leftovers to our families, friends, and to God.

The next two levels of the pyramid deal with esteem needs and self-actualization. I am not even going to go into them because many of us have failed to establish a firm foundation regarding the needs that we have already discussed. At this point, I hope you have given some serious thought to what it means to "provide for your family." We have a responsibility to provide so much more than simply wealth and status. If you can provide for all of your family's needs while generating wealth, good for you. However, if you neglect your family and they are suffering because of your pursuit to provide for them solely on a financial basis, then you are far from meeting their needs. You might want to consider the possibility that you are failing them because of your addiction to success.

Improving Our Workplace

Promotions and transfers usually lead to the gratifying experience of people telling you how much better things became after you arrived. Another way in which this emotion manifests itself is when people sense that you may be leaving and attempt to guilt you into staying. They use comments like, "I don't know what we would do without you," "You're the only reason I'm still here," or the more direct, "Please don't leave us!" While it may be satisfying to know that people need and appreciate you, this is actually a symptom of a problem rather than a complement.

Let's suppose that these comments are genuine and not just the efforts of an individual eager to win your appreciation. Maybe you instituted new policies or processes, you improved employee morale, or you eliminated inefficient practices so that people could spend more time doing what they do best. All of these are wonderful accomplishments but you have to ask yourself why no one acted on these issues before you came along. I believe there are three primary reasons:

1. They did not possess the knowledge or skills of how to make the changes.
2. They had the knowledge and skills, but lacked the empowerment to make the changes.
3. Some people just like to have a reason to complain.

Let's look at each of these situations and how you can handle them. My intention is not to go deeply into management techniques, but the issue of feeling guilty or selfish about pursuing our passions is a common one. I just want to touch on a few of the sources of this guilt to get you to think from a practical standpoint about what you need to do to move into a different role or shift your focus in your current role without leaving your coworkers stranded.

Lack of Knowledge or Skills

The first situation is easy to remedy. If people rely on us for our knowledge and skills, then it is our duty to educate them. Have you ever worked with an individual who guards their knowledge? You know this person. They have usually been in their position for several years and selectively release fragments of their knowledge only when it will make them look good or someone else look bad. Do not be this person! They define their success by their ability to drop strategically placed knowledge-bombs in order to make themselves look better by comparison. As we have already seen, this is not success but low self-esteem.

If you feel imprisoned by a particular job because no one else can do it as well as you or because others lack the intimate knowledge that you have, you are sadly mistaken. While it may be true that you are very talented at dealing with the conglomeration of all that your job entails, I would venture to say that you could find someone else who can perform each of the individual aspects of your job better than you can. If your desire is to break free of your imprisonment, one of your top priorities needs to be identifying and grooming individuals to take over specific responsibilities after you are gone. Not only will this make your departure easier, but also it will be enriching to those individuals as they gain new experience and greater levels of responsibility. Just make sure that the responsibilities that they undertake are in line with their passions so you don't imprison them as you break free.

Another possible result of sharing your knowledge and developing others is that doing so can allow you to delegate some of your responsibilities. As you do this, you may realize that you are able to free up enough time and energy to pursue your mission without quitting your current job or changing careers. Freeing yourself from your self-imposed prison of success ultimately means escaping a mindset. This may require changing employers or starting a new career, but that is not an absolute. Some of you may be in the perfect job to pursue your passions; you have just been focusing your efforts in the wrong areas. By delegating those responsibilities that prevent the pursuit of your passions and changing the way that you define success, you could find that a drastic career change is unnecessary.

You may be wondering what all of this has to do with escaping from the imprisonment of false success. Remember that we measure false success by money, power, and recognition. Because many of us are seeking more power and recognition, we either intentionally or subconsciously attempt to keep the most important and glamorous responsibilities for ourselves. These responsibilities may not be in the areas we are passionate about, but we are afraid to give them up because to do so may allow someone else gain more power and recognition. As a result, we continue to devote ourselves to responsibilities we are dispassionate about, thus preventing the pursuit of our mission. In the end, our striving for false success circumvents the attainment of true success because of our unwillingness to delegate key responsibilities to others who may even be better suited to accept them. We are often the prison guard of our own prison—all we have to do is use the key and open the door.

Lack of Empowerment

The second situation is a little bit tougher because it involves a cultural change. We toss the word "empowerment" around quite liberally in our business culture. There are mountains of books available that tell you to empower your employees by driving decision-making as far down the organizational chart as possible, but I think empowerment is only effective when accompanied by encouragement. The root word of empowerment is *power*. Power is synonymous with strength, fortitude, and force. However, in most business settings, managers chastise employees when they make an error in judgment, resulting in timidity. Timidity is an absence of courage, and courage happens to be the root of *encouragement*. Therefore, without encouragement, there can be no empowerment.

This is the downward spiral that often occurs in business. An organization has a culture of micromanagement with little or no reward for courage. A well-intentioned but ill-informed group of managers realizes that they are making all of the decisions and dictating them to employees. This group of managers decides that the employees need to be empowered so that they can make their own decisions, which will result in more buy-in and commitment. The managers hold a meeting and tell the employees that they are now empowered and they may go forth on their decision-making adventures. The managers smile and nod approvingly while the employees leave the meeting confused.

There are two problems with this approach. First, if the culture has been that of micromanagement (the absence of

55

empowerment), it is likely that managers drag people through the coals whenever problems arise. In these types of cultures, the first question asked when a problem arises is not "What happened?" but "Whose idea was this?" A few rounds of finger pointing ensue until the most powerful faction identifies a satisfactory scapegoat and puts the situation to rest. There is no reward for the risk taken nor is there any attempt to understand the intricacies of the problem and the lessons learned from it. There is only blame and discouragement. After people have seen this play out a few times, they are far too timid to make decisions on their own. They feel they must get a powerful manager to back them before going forward with their ideas. That is why managers receive at least a hundred cyrcc's (cover your rear complimentary copies) of emails every day. The fear of making a mistake paralyzes people to the point that they are content to carry on with the status quo, however inefficient, wasteful, and debilitating it may be.

The second problem with this approach is simple. If you have to tell people that they are empowered, then they most assuredly are not. That is why encouragement is so important to fostering empowerment. If you continually encourage people and help them to view their failures as learning experiences, they soon learn that it is acceptable to make a mistake as long as they learn from it and take steps to correct it. Of course, you should not coddle your employees either. Your goal is to get people to want to make decisions based on what they believe is right, rather than what they believe will make the fewest waves.

Too often, excellence—from solutions based on what is right—is sacrificed for adequacy—from solutions based on what will ruffle the fewest feathers. We chose an 80 percent chance of adequacy over a 50 percent chance of excellence because we lack courage. I think this is because our business culture teaches us to focus on the prevention of failure. We interpret a 50 percent chance of excellence as being synonymous with a 50 percent chance of failure. In the same way, we will equate an 80 percent chance of adequacy with a 20 percent chance of failure. Because the chances of failure are lower, we choose adequacy. We don't consider that even failure in the pursuit of excellence may lead to a better result than successfully achieving adequacy. This parallels the choices we make with our lives and careers as we seek the safest way to prevent what we perceive as career or life failure rather than pursuing the chance of discovering excellence through the pursuit of our passions.

Some People Just Like to Have a Reason to Complain

You know this person. They complain about you and everything you try to do. You would think that they would be happy with your departure, but when they hear you are leaving or delegating key responsibilities, they complain about that as well. This person just likes to have a reason to complain. This is an immature approach to life and if you let this person's complaints dictate the decisions you make, you are only sustaining their immaturity.

Pursuing your mission requires a great deal of personal leadership. Will there be people upset along the way? You bet! In fact, any cause that does not create tension, draw criticism, and raise a few brows is probably not meaningful enough to be your personal mission. Just make sure you are pursuing the right mission, you are fully committed to that mission, it is in accordance with your values, and you are pursuing it to the best of your ability. If you believe in what you are doing and have assurance in the need to do it, you will be more prepared to endure a naysayer or two along the way. I can assure you that no matter what you do with your life, there will be someone somewhere criticizing the way you do it. You might as well face that criticism while doing something about which you are passionate.

Chapter 3–What About Fulfillment?

Throughout our careers, much of our focus is on success and getting to the next level. We spend our time and effort preoccupied with *how* to get there rather than stopping to ask *why* or even *if* we want to go to the next level. When we talk about career ambition, we relate it to promotions and perceived success (money, power, and recognition). We view those who relentlessly struggle to get ahead as great ambassadors of success. In reality, this mentality of succeeding at all costs is not career ambition at all. It is success ambition. True career ambition results when you know your values and spend every day doing something meaningful to further your mission. Who do you think has more ambition for their career—the middle manager who receives a nice paycheck and benefits for performing a job that has little to do with their values or the missionary who receives little or no financial incentive, but gets to see lives transformed on a regular basis?

A paycheck is not the only thing we get from going to work everyday. Far more important than any size paycheck is a sense of fulfillment. This fulfillment comes through the relationships that we build, the legacy that we leave, and by focusing on what we do rather than what we have. From my experience in the business world, there are legions of people who claim to be successful but lack fulfillment.

What Kind of Relationships Am I Building?

When you really think about it, the essence of life comes down to relationships. These relationships can be broken down into three main categories: our relationship with ourselves, our relationship with others, and our relationship with God. I believe we will never achieve true fulfillment until each of these relationships is healthy. The problem for most of us is that we prefer to focus on tasks and assignments that we believe will lead to success rather than relationships. We place our quest for success ahead of understanding our own mission (our relationship with ourselves); we often regard a relationship with a coworker only for its ability to advance our quest for success, and many of us who have a relationship with God attempt to separate our "spiritual" life from our "professional" life.

Our Relationship with Ourselves

I have to admit, whenever I hear a phrase like "our relationship with ourselves," I have a tendency to roll my eyes and brace myself for an insipid discussion on self-esteem and how we are all winners if we just find ourselves and accept who we are. Yes, there are some people who have low self-esteem and just need to have a more realistic view of their abilities, but there are also many in the business world who have an over-inflated self-esteem. They believe that because they get a fat paycheck and have a high level of responsibility, they are more important to society and are greater contributors than someone who defines success as pursuing their passions and fulfilling their mission.

This is another one of the dangers of false success. Once we obtain significant amounts of those indicators of false success, society tells us we are doing the right thing and we just need to keep plugging away. As we continue to focus on those efforts that bring us false success, we become more deeply entrenched and it becomes more difficult to escape. This is why it is important for us to have a good relationship with ourselves and understand what true success means to us.

I think we all have an internal gauge that knows when we are doing something of real importance as opposed to just letting life pass by. I understood early in my career that my lack of experience and maturity meant that much of my work would focus on areas of less importance and I would find more significance in my work as I advanced through my career. I thought that explained why I felt destined to do something else and figured I should just wait it out until I reached a level of success that would bring significance with it. Numerous promotions came; I made more money, gained more power, and grew in recognition. The importance of my work had increased substantially, but my internal monitor told me that the significance was still not there.

Don't get me wrong; there were many significant aspects to my career. I formed key relationships, completed important projects, and I gained invaluable experience and maturity. Yet despite my career growth, I still felt as if I was in the passenger seat of this vehicle of success watching my life pass by on the other side of the windows. I was waiting for a sense of significance to come to me rather than getting out of the vehicle and seeking it myself.

Eventually, I mounted the courage to listen to that inner voice and I stepped away from the false success. Although some people could not understand why I would do such a thing, the overwhelming majority of people understood completely. Some, who were more successful in the false sense, even seemed a bit envious. At that point, I had only revealed my internal conflict with the pursuit of false success to a few people. If few people understood my internal conflict, how could the others be so understanding and supportive? I believe it is because many of us struggle with the conflict between false success and significance, yet few of us choose significance over success. When someone we know actually steps out and makes the commitment to seek significance, we feel vindicated in our own feelings. This all goes back to our relationship with our self. If we fail to listen to ourselves and blindly follow the path to false success, then significance and fulfillment will only be a daydream that permeates our subconscious and leaves us conflicted and incomplete.

Our Relationship with Others

If relationships are so important, why do we spend so little time tending to them? For most of us, we would rather focus on tasks than on relationships. This is particularly true in our professional lives. We go about our everyday routine plowing through the tasks rather than taking the time to put some effort into our relationships. These tasks may be reports, regular meetings, or ongoing projects with no end in sight. We complain about how mundane the tasks are or how boring the meetings are, yet we cling to them to prevent us from doing something uncomfortable like really getting to know our coworkers. We view our coworkers as partners enlisted to help us objectively solve problems in the workplace. While there is a level of satisfaction that results from working with other people to solve task-related problems, this has little lasting impact on our lives or theirs.

We form true relationships when we drop our guard and let others see our honest self. Again, this goes against the practical everyday teachings throughout most of Corporate America, which tells us not to take things personally and to keep our poker face on when emotions flare. We believe that showing emotion is a sign of weakness or lack of control. While I am definitely not an advocate for bawling your eyes out over every issue at work, I think it is a mistake to show no emotion at all.

The emotions that you show are an outward expression of the passion within you. Some people are uncomfortable with this, so rather than displaying a passion for their work, they focus on the tasks. By making their work task-oriented and snuffing out their passion, they are making fulfillment almost impossible to attain.

Why do we turn to tasks for comfort? For starters, tasks are easier to manage. They have quantifiable parameters and a finishing point. Tasks do not have feelings or opinions of their own. Tasks rarely require us to change who we are or how we interact with them. Relationships, by contrast, are much more complex. You cannot say you have reached a goal in a relationship by accomplishing scheduled milestones. Relationships are constantly changing and growing. Relationships sometimes require us to change who we are and how we think. In fact, any relationship that does not require a significant amount of sacrifice is not much of a relationship at all.

So if relationships are so important, why do we put so little effort into them on a daily basis? I think the reason is because we live in a "me" culture. By that, I do not mean that we are always looking out for ourselves and focusing on our own welfare. Many generous people in the world freely give of their time and resources to help others. The "me" culture to which I am referring is the culture of self-reliance and independence we have developed, particularly amongst young professionals. We think we have to achieve wealth, success, and happiness on our own and any outside help we receive is a sign of weakness. We admire those who are "self-made." In truth, those who have reached their accomplishments through collaboration and the support of others are the people who get the most satisfaction in life. In the end, the self-made success stories have nothing left but their accomplishments, while those who accept support often have lasting friendships.

Some of the most truly successful people in the world did not achieve their success because of their intelligence or skills, but because of their understanding of the importance of relationships. Think about the people you know. If someone shuns your help as they set out to make it on their own, do you really care if they succeed? You may not want them to fail, but you are probably not committed to their success. On the other hand, if a person shows you that they are passionate about an issue and they come to you seeking your assistance, your outlook will probably be different.

Take this a step further and imagine that the person seeking success is someone who really knows you. They know what makes you laugh, what ticks you off, and what inspires you. Furthermore, you know they would be there for you in a second if you were in need. If this is the case, you will probably be totally committed to that individual's success and will do everything within reason to help them.

Flip that scenario around and imagine that you are the person in need of assistance. How many people do you really know at work? Do you know their passions? Do they know yours? Do they know that you would be there for them if they were in need? If you cannot think of some key people immediately, you have some relationship building to do.

Relationship building is simply not a focus in most work environments. Our business mindset has been to focus on the issues and to guard our emotions. If we make any friends along the way, that's great, but it is not our primary objective. We focus on numbers like financial results, customer return rates, and sales volumes. What the majority of the business world fails to realize is that while it is difficult—if not impossible—to measure how well we are doing at building relationships, the results of relationship building are absolutely quantifiable.

If your facility has experienced a significant improvement in production, the vice president of your division does not want to hear that it came about because of an improved relationship between a manufacturing engineer and a production supervisor who could never see eye-to-eye before. They want to hear about how well the new four million dollar machine is running. They want to hear about how someone modified the data acquisition system on the machine to detect a specific type of defect that was previously causing the yields to be low. In truth, improvements on this machine never would have materialized if the relationship between those key contributors had not first improved. We ignore this fact and instead of congratulating the individuals for working together, we applaud their technical expertise. To these people, this just reinforces the misconception that tasks are more important than relationships.

Because of this practical reinforcement, we focus on the wrong things at work, leaving us unfulfilled. When a problem arises at work, we all have opinions on how to handle it, yet many lack the relational foundation necessary to listen to others, respect their opinions, and collaborate to get to the best solution. Instead, we believe that our way is the best way and we go to battle at the conference table defending our opinions while repudiating the thoughts of others. Eventually all sides involved make a sufficient number of concessions to allow for a solution that nobody likes, but still contains the components that each party was most adamant about. The result is certainly not the best solution for the problem—it may not even be a good solution. Instead, it is the negotiated compromise of a group of people unwilling to devote as much energy into building relationships as they do to arguing their opinions.

If this sounds similar to how your organization approaches problem solving, then you know the frustration that comes from focusing on tasks and problems rather than relationship building. I challenge you to shift your focus. If you make your relationship with others a priority over arguing your opinion, you stand a much better chance of having your opinion fall on receptive ears. With some people, this will be extremely difficult because of their personality or lack thereof. Your objective with these individuals is to find some sort of connection; some common ground to focus on which to build your relationship.

It is also important to keep in mind that every single person on this planet does something better than you. Likewise, every person you meet has a mission. Whether they have surrendered to that mission or not, they have a burning desire for something. Your relationship with them will be stronger if you understand and respect that mission because it may just explain the bias through which they see the world and the rationale behind their opinions. Once we understand that a person's opposition to our ideas is not because they simply want to oppose us, but because they truly believe their methods will result in the best solution, it is easier to listen to them and collaborate with them rather than compromise.

Our Relationship with God

Our self-reliant culture has not only limited the extent to which we build relationships with other people, it has also widened the gap between our society and God. Even many of the people who claim to have a relationship with God are very reluctant to place their trust fully in Him. As a Christian, I believe that God gives us our mission in life. He grants us specific talents and gifts to accomplish our mission, puts key people in our lives so we may foster relationships to further our mission, and grants us life experiences (both good and bad) to better equip us to fulfill our mission. He also places that burning desire in our hearts to want to carry out the mission He has planned for us. I believe this is what causes the feeling of frustration in the lack of significance in your work, and the deep-seated belief that there is something more to your life.

Despite all God does to prepare us to pursue our mission (the talents, skills, relationships, experiences, and passions He gives us), and despite the fact that He is all-knowing, all-powerful, and all-present, He leaves us a choice. He grants us a free will to choose whether we will pursue our mission. Many of us, Christians included, denounce the sovereignty of God daily as we chose to pursue the false success defined by society rather than the true success that comes from the pursuit of our mission. We know that we feel led to do something more meaningful with our lives but with typical self-interest, we decide that we are better judges of our life circumstances than God Himself. Instead, we decide to follow a predictable, safe route leading to empty success. We have our own agenda and if it is convenient to glorify God along the way, we'll try to work that in as time allows.

We may even take this a step further by commending our perseverance as we overcome obstacles to achieve whatever level of "success" we attain. It is only when we have a close relationship with God that we can understand that there is a reason for our obstacles. Authentically understanding and trusting in the sovereignty of God is difficult for believers and nonbelievers alike. We seem to place our faith in God only when we feel it will improve our status in the world or help us move in the direction that we think is best. We think that we always know what is best for us and get frustrated when God doesn't seem to be on board with our plans.

We have to accept the fact that there will be times when we do not understand how God works. Bad things happen all the time and they will continue to happen. There will be natural disasters, homes lost in fires, terrible automobile accidents, terrorist attacks, the death of loved ones, financial difficulties, health problems; the list continues indefinitely. Some people question why God would allow these things to occur. If God is all-powerful, why does He not just put an end to the suffering that is going on around the world? The problem with that question is that we are trying to put ourselves in God's place. Since the Garden of Eden, man and woman have desired to achieve the same level of knowledge and discernment as God. To this very day, we have the fallible tendency to think that we know ourselves better than God does and are quite capable of making important life decisions without His help.

Rather than accept that God is sovereign and that all of His ways will be revealed to us if we trust in Him, we question His motives and wonder whether or not He is listening to our pleas. In the same way that we question His sovereignty when it comes to the suffering in the world, we also question His sovereignty when it comes to our mission in life. We ignore the need to change our focus and forego opportunities to pursue our mission, telling ourselves that our lives are just too busy right now and we'll be able to pursue our passions and listen to God when things calm down a bit. We're too busy right now? We are forcing ourselves through another day of insignificance and discontent so we can continue to enjoy our "success" which we already know leaves us unfulfilled! Is that what we are busy doing?

What is My Legacy?

I believe that leaving a legacy is a hallmark of great leaders, yet so few people in leadership positions are working toward that goal. This is probably due to our prioritization of tasks over relationships. If we intend to leave a lasting legacy, our priority needs to be people. A true legacy results when we fundamentally influence the way people think and act. Because of this, leaving a legacy entails a great deal of responsibility.

Simply leaving a legacy is not necessarily a good thing. Countless leaders throughout history have changed the way people thought and acted, but they did so in a way that was detrimental to society. If we wish to leave a positive legacy, we first have to understand our values and core beliefs. If we fail to understand our values, all of our work is meaningless because deep down, values are what give us our passion. Without passion, we cannot motivate others into action. Without motivating others into action, we cannot influence culture. Without influencing culture, we cannot leave a legacy.

Some may try to leave a legacy only because that is what the latest leadership book they read told them to do. Their focus is entirely on themselves and their success. They want to be a good leader and good leaders leave a legacy; therefore, they decide they will leave their legacy, check that box, then move on to the next agenda. Because they have not really given much thought to their values nor the things that they are passionate about, they select a generic initiative they are dispassionate about and force it down people's throats until their followers submit and are assimilated. Their goal is not to create a legacy based on their passions, but rather a legacy that proves their worthiness as a leader.

This is a little over the top, but you get the idea and can probably think of individuals who are not too far from this description. The key here is that if you want to leave a true legacy, you first have to understand what you are passionate about, then you have to find other people who can link their passions to your mission, and finally you have to be unfaltering in your pursuit of that mission. Be careful with how you interpret that last sentence. Unfaltering does not mean that we will never make mistakes or that we will never fall short of our goals. It means that we are steadfast and unrelenting as we pursue those goals.

If you are in a leadership position and you do not align your daily efforts with your values, then you are failing miserably as a leader. That sounds harsh, but it is true. It is also a bitter reality for many of us. I can't begin to tell you how many times I filled out my daily task list in the morning intent on implementing changes and devising strategies that were in harmony with my values, only to have them swept away in the whirlwind of the average, chaotic day. Many of my peers gave up completely, choosing not make out any plans for the day and holding up their catcher's mitt ready for the next fastball (or curveball) coming their way.

No legacy is worth leaving if we do not understand why we are leaving it, yet many of us go to work everyday without an understanding of where we are, what we want to do, or where we want to be. We have deadlines, mandates, and directives that filter down to us, leaving us with little time or energy to focus on what really matters.

Another mistake we make is that most of us think of leaving a legacy in the context of our careers, but that is just one slice of the pie. We must live out our values at home, as well. It is important to understand where we have the greatest level of influence. Notice that I didn't say that we need to understand where we have the most power. Only those who want it to continue after you are gone will propagate your legacy. That is why influence is more effective than power when it comes to leaving a legacy.

For many, the area in our lives where we have the most influence is with our families. While this seems like an obvious place for us to leave a legacy, many people focus on influencing their workplace while neglecting their families all for the sake of their perception of success. You don't get any promotions or raises for the time and effort that you put into leading your family, but the sense of fulfillment will be more rewarding.

You may be thinking that this does not pertain to you. You spend time with the kids, you listen to your spouse, and you would do anything for the wellbeing of your family. However, ask yourself this question: If you were never to see your family again, what have you done lately that will positively affect their decisions years from now? If you cannot come up with some specific examples, it is time for you to reevaluate your priorities.

Because you are reading this book, you probably have some doubts about where you have been concentrating your efforts. You have likely been so busy with your career that the mere concept of doing something meaningful outside of your job seems foreign. You feel pressured into pouring yourself into the pursuit of success, but you know that there is something more to life than a paycheck and a promotion. I cannot tell you what that thing is because it is different for all of us. What I can tell you is that if you do not prioritize your life so you can focus on what you feel is truly important, you will never fulfill your purpose, and true success will always be beyond your grasp. Sure, you may obtain success as defined by others, but that will be of little consolation to you as you struggle to find fulfillment.

People are always observing you and learning from you. Some of those people are the ones that you know and love, such as your family, while others may be mere acquaintances. Think about what you are teaching them. Are you leaving behind a legacy based on deeply held convictions, or are you loosely flying through life setting a spectacular example of how not to live?

Doing Versus Having

Another one of the reasons so many of us lack fulfillment is because we focus too much on what we have (or want to have) and too little on what we do. I am not just referring to what we have materialistically. It may be the job title that we have, the education that we have, the type of office that we have, or the respect that we have. We think of results as goals in and of themselves. When we do this, we shortchange the process by which we should be attaining those goals.

Consider education: if someone were to ask you what your goals were for your education while you were a student, what would your answer have been? It probably would have been something along the lines of obtaining a degree, maybe with a certain grade point average, and possibly within a specific timeframe. Very few people would answer this question by saying that they want to gain intimate knowledge regarding a specific subject so they can utilize their knowledge to make new breakthroughs in their field.

We view the diploma itself as a goal—a ticket to a better life. True to our success-obsessed culture, we seek to obtain that ticket as quickly as possible. This usually means taking the easiest path we can. For those of you who have a college degree, I want you to think back to those ever popular "humanities electives" that you took your sophomore year. It is a safe bet that

Music Appreciation was a more popular elective course than Anthropology. Is that because students have a deep desire to learn about the various styles of music and want to gain a better knowledge of the classical composers? No, it is because they think the Music Appreciation class will be an easier way to achieve their goal—a college degree.

Further evidence of the circumvention of the learning process is the prevalence of cheating in schools. According to a 2002 study of twelve thousand students cited by ABC News[4], 74 percent of the high school students admitted to cheating at least once in the previous year. While there are numerous reasons for this, near the top of the list is the pressure to succeed. Children are pushed to make good grades because that is their parents' interpretation of success. Many well-meaning parents place more emphasis on the results (grades) than the process (learning). Oh sure, there are some students who are intellectually gifted, some who are very diligent, and some who are a combination of the two, but there are also some who simply know how to work the system. They can fake the appearance of success by cheating.

Now apply this to the business world. Do you have an annual goal-planning session with your manager? It usually works something like this. Prior to you ever meeting with your manager, a laundry list of improvements was given to them by their manager, which was given to them by their manager, which was given to them their manager, who happens to have no clue who you are or what you do. Each item of the list continues to flow downward through the organizational chart until it finally meets squarely with a person who can actually do something to

---

[4] ABC News, "A Cheating Crisis in America's Schools," http://abcnews.go.com/Primetime/story?id=132376

make it happen. Your manager then presents this "opportunity" to you as one of your annual objectives. The obvious problem with this system is that it fails to take into consideration an individual's talents, skills, and developmental needs. Additionally, what we routinely discuss as *goals* are actually *results*. You have seen these before—reduce waste by 5 percent... improve efficiency to 98 percent... reduce our customer return rate to 0.01 percent. You may even have something very similar to this as your objectives right now. These are not objectives at all. They are the results of the organized efforts of groups of people.

Think of it this way. If your "goal" is to lose ten pounds, you cannot wake up every morning, repeat aloud "I will lose ten pounds today" while eating breakfast, and expect your gut to disappear. Losing weight is a result. The goals associated with obtaining that result should be limiting your diet to a set number of calories or running a specific number of miles each week.

Let us draw the parallel to education. Just as the process of learning (what we do) is neglected because of our focus on grades (what we have), so also is the process of lasting improvement because of our focus on "hitting the numbers." Just as we saw in the education example, there are people in the business world who are intellectually gifted, others who are diligent, and some who are a combination of the two, but some simply know how to work the system. I am sure you can think of people who would fit into the latter group. When it comes to their entire management arsenal, they couldn't muster enough firepower to battle a crate of puppies, but because they focused on the right buzzword at the right time, their manager viewed them as a hero. The reward for their ability to focus on the hot item of the month while completely neglecting long-term improvement is continual promotions and raises. This results in more money, more power, more recognition, and the propagation of the myth that these very things are the results of success. Due to the amount of money, power, and recognition these individuals have amassed, other people shower them with admiration for their "accomplishments," thus reinforcing their own false perception of their success.

We can expand this beyond the individual level. Look at what happened with publicly traded companies in the late 1990s and early 2000s. Investors played the role of parents pressuring organizations to get good grades. Some companies decided they were willing to risk long-term sustained growth in order to show the numbers demanded by investors. Entire organizations were guilty of "cheating" so they could "get a good grade." We all know how that story ends.

Whether we are talking about an individual or an entire organization, the message is the same. We can focus on short-term success and produce the numbers that we know will demand approval, but the actual lasting impact we have will be minimal. We may even fool ourselves into believing that this false success is a great achievement, but we will never find fulfillment in our careers as long as we focus on what we have because we will always desire more. Whether it is more money, more power, or more success itself, we will never have enough. What we have now is only the baseline for the next level of success, which is why people have such difficulty taking a job that pays less or gives them less power. Unfortunately for people with this mindset, that may be exactly what they need to do in order to find fulfillment.

True fulfillment in our careers will only come to those who focus on what they do, rather than what they have. God gave us specific skills, talents, interests, and values. If you talk to someone who finds fulfillment in their career, it is usually because they get to spend most of their time utilizing them. Little time needs to be wasted worrying about results when we are performing a job in which we have a great deal of talent. Instead, we can become engrossed in the process and find a deeper level of satisfaction that could never come from "hitting the numbers." Look at gifted artists or musicians. They do not judge their work by how it looks or sounds but by how it feels to them. In fact, their uniqueness is frequently what sets them apart as being gifted rather than simply talented. It may be time for you to stop judging your career based on how it looks or sounds and start judging it by how it feels.

Of course, not all of us are fortunate enough to have a career that is in alignment with our talents. You have bills to pay, mouths to feed, college savings accounts, and a 401(k) to fund. If you find yourself in this situation, the first step is to ask yourself if you really need all you think that you need. Next, think about what you have to gain by freeing yourself of those things that you do not really need. Once you accept the fact that none of the extraneous junk you can accumulate defines success, you will begin to head down the road to freedom.

Your career is a trade-off. You give your employer your time, skills, and knowledge in return for money, benefits, and hopefully some level of satisfaction. When broken down to the most basic level, we can think of this as a trade-off in which we earn an income in return for our time. There is an exchange of two resources—time and money. Of these two, time is by far more precious. You will never recover time once it has been lost nor can you bank time in hopes of compounding its value. Each individual determines the value placed on his or her time. When we accept a job offer, I believe we are essentially accepting the income and benefits offered as the value that we place on our time. Because of this view, we are setting ourselves up for some serious frustration. The problem here is that we have neglected to take into account the exchange of our skills and knowledge for job satisfaction.

You may think that your skills and knowledge play an integral role in determining the value of your time and in deciding your income when a job offer comes along. While there is some truth to this, it is also true that there are a lot of highly skilled, highly knowledgeable, highly paid individuals who feel completely underutilized because their daily activities have nothing to do with their talents and strengths. We are all guilty of getting so involved in the useless minutia that it would appear we have completely forgotten the value of our time only to complain later about not having enough of it.

Regardless of how much a job pays, you will not find fulfillment unless you deploy your skills and knowledge in a manner that is in alignment with your values. This does not mean that you should quit your job immediately and join the Peace Corps. You should take the time to understand what motivates you and come to terms with the fact that the elements that comprise your motivation and the elements that make up other people's perception of your success are not the same. In fact, the pursuit of a career that you believe will bring you success may be taking you further away from what you really need to do with your life in order to find fulfillment.

Do not let "success" be the enemy of your mission in life. Yes, your life has a mission. I know many people have a hard time grasping this notion. They think the whole concept of a life-mission is gung-ho motivational rhetoric, but that is because they have never surrendered themselves to their mission. Either we wrap ourselves up so much in what we call success that we fail to find out what our mission truly is, or we go through life pretending to be blissfully ignorant of our mission because we fear what it may require of us. We stay in our comfort zone so we can continue to be successful, because sometimes being successful is actually the easiest route. I know this is contrary to what most of us believe, but it takes real courage and effort to step away from what we know is safe in order to pursue something that captivates us. Many of us focus so much on what we can have that we become completely oblivious to what we can do.

I must issue a word of caution here. By focusing on what we can do, we should not take this to the point of believing that our actions alone will redeem our spirits and give us ultimate fulfillment. Begrudgingly volunteering our services to a cause for which we have no passion will lead to burnout, not fulfillment. Too many people who are trying to do what is right are doing so out of discipline rather than desire. They want to check the boxes on those areas in their lives that they think will bring approval from others. We may be able to fool others, but we cannot fool ourselves nor can we fool God, and that is where we can find fulfillment—not from the approval of others.

As I said before, the fulfillment that comes from focusing on what we do will only be achieved when our actions are in accordance with our beliefs. This deceptively simple truth evades many of us because we have such a vague understanding of our own beliefs and how they apply to our everyday life. We may have heartfelt beliefs on religion, family, and our roles in the lives of others, but we tend to put up partitions that delineate these separate lives. As a result, we turn to the collective beliefs of those around us to define what it is that we want to accomplish. If we are to live in accordance to our beliefs, it is essential that we merge all areas of our life and live under the same set of rules all of the time.

By now, I hope you realize that true fulfillment has absolutely nothing to do with the metrics that our society uses to measure success. This is not to say that those metrics of success are the antithesis of fulfillment. It is entirely possible to have wealth, power, and recognition and still have fulfillment. However, we must remember that our fulfillment does not result from those indicators that our society uses to define success. I think true fulfillment comes from:

- Having a good relationship with ourselves, others, and God
- Utilizing these relationships to make a lasting positive impact on others
- Understanding our mission and how it relates to those relationships
- Focusing on what we can do to make that mission a reality and not just a daydream
- Leaving a legacy so that others can continue to propagate our mission after we are gone

Now think about where you are focusing your efforts. I am sure you work very hard and endure a great deal of frustration in order to achieve what the world calls success. Do your daily tasks and achievements have anything to do with the five items listed above? Is it any wonder that we have such a hard time finding fulfillment? Is it any surprise that we are not satisfied with success?

Chapter 4–Ladders and Dog Races

In this chapter, I use a couple of analogies to illustrate our unceasing efforts to gain more success. The whole idea is not to shun success or marginalize those who are successful. My goal is to get you to think about what you are striving to attain and, more importantly, why. You would think that smart, talented, diligent professionals would understand exactly what they want and why they want it; however, it has been my observation that this is not the case. I have seen a several successful professionals who are miserable with what they do everyday—not because they lack "success," but because they continue to follow a path that leads them away from their passions. Yet for some reason, they continue along their path of success—widening the gap between themselves and their passion.

Climbing Ladders

The good, old corporate ladder—it is a symbol of advancement, growth, and success. It has many milestones along the way and our relative position on it is a testament to our hard work and dedication. Moreover, ladders are useful tools. Climbing a ladder allows us to reach places that otherwise are beyond our grasp and see things that are out of our view from the ground. If you have a ladder at home, undoubtedly you have used it for these reasons, but have you ever taken your ladder out, set it up, and repeatedly climbed it solely for the sake of climbing a ladder? Unless you have a bizarre workout regimen, the answer is probably "no."

When we use a ladder, we use it as a tool to elevate ourselves—allowing us to perform a task that we would not be able to accomplish from the ground. Look to the business world, however, and you will see that many of us spend our entire careers climbing the corporate ladder simply for the sake of climbing higher up the ladder.

This may have started when we were children in school. Our success-obsessed culture told us that in order to be of greater worth relative to other students, we had to make good grades. This was our way of demonstrating to others that we had what it took to be successful. Later as we progressed through high school, our grades represented something more than just a vehicle through which we could make our parents proud and classmates envious. We then began to strive to make good grades so that we could gain acceptance into the best colleges and possibly even earn scholarships.

During our junior and senior years of high school, we begin to make decisions about where to go to college, what major to study, and how to spend the remainder of our professional lives. At this point in our professional development, we have about as clear of an understanding of our long-term career path as we have of the tax advantages of a Roth IRA. All we see is the next rung on the ladder and we know that we want to be standing on it.

After we get into college, at some point our attention turns to life after school. Some people take longer than others, but we are the aggressive, driven type so we begin thinking about this early in college. We push to be successful in college so we will be able to compete for the top jobs once we graduate. Again, we just want to keep climbing the ladder that extends endlessly above us and promises a brighter future with each step.

For most of us, a college degree means an entry-level job where we can gain some real world experience. After a bit of floundering due to actual work being nothing like the concrete, textbook problems to which we were accustomed in college, the successful people aspire to exceed the expectations of others so that they can take on more responsibility and pull themselves up to that next step.

At this early stage in a career, we often lack an intimate knowledge of systems and the politics surrounding our projects. We just know that our boss has given us an objective and if we blow it out of the water, we may set ourselves up for future opportunities. Furthermore, we do not spend much time contemplating how our responsibilities fit in with our overall mission. We believe there will be time for that sort of thing later on after the promotions and raises materialize. Besides, we think that if we bog ourselves down with a personal mission, we may miss a key assignment that could help bolster us up the ladder.

Eventually, we earn those promotions that we so desired and take on greater responsibilities. This process repeats itself and after a few iterations, we find that we have climbed to a considerable height on the ladder. Rather than evaluate where we are, we gaze longingly at the rung above us and start reaching. Many of us are so busy hastily climbing that we fail to recognize that we really have no idea where this ladder leads. Furthermore, we are too intent on getting further up the ladder to take inventory of our decisions made earlier in life.

We make some of our most important long-term decisions when we are immature and ignorant of our mission. That in itself is not that bad—we have to get started somewhere and it is good learn what does and does not work for us rather than procrastinate. On the other hand, we cannot expect a senior in high school to know exactly what college major to study and career to choose in order to facilitate a life of fulfillment and significance. The tragedy occurs when we have too much pride and stubbornness to admit that we are on the wrong ladder. We choose to keep climbing in hopes that our height on the ladder will overcome our frustration with being on the wrong one.

Right now, you may know that the ladder you are climbing is not right for you. The view is not as good as you thought it would be and the things that you can now reach do not bring the happiness you originally believed they would—but you keep telling yourself that once you reach the next step, you will be happy. You probably have thoughts like these: if I can just get that next promotion, I will have fulfillment; or, if I can just make a certain amount of money, I will be satisfied. Almost without fail, when you get that next promotion or raise, you are content for a short amount of time, and then you start looking up the ladder to see where you can go next. You feel as if your discontentment with your position is a result how high you are on the ladder rather than your initial choice of ladder. Because of this, you just keep reaching higher in an attempt to fill the void within yourself with the temporary pleasure of false success. What a foolish way to waste your life! At some point, you have to realize that all of these steps lead to the same destination. If the destination is wrong, it does not matter how high you climb—you are on the wrong ladder.

Don't get me wrong, there is nothing inherently bad about climbing ladders. Just make sure that you are on the right one. While you may think that getting to that next rung will bring you happiness, if you are on the wrong ladder, that step will only take you further from the ground, and unless you possess the aerial acrobatics of a squirrel, the only way to get to another ladder is by returning to the ground. Unfortunately, many have forgotten about the ground because they are staring intently on what lies above. Now they are no longer prisoners to their current success, but also prisoners to the prospect of the success that they may someday achieve. This is not to say that we should forgo our dreams and aspirations, we just need to understand what those dreams and aspirations really are. Unless you are a greedy, gluttonous, power-hungry egomaniac, your true aspirations in life probably have little to do with whether or not you keep climbing higher up that ladder.

It is also important to realize that what we incorrectly consider ambition is sometimes nothing more than a resignation to live a life of predictability and comfort perched high upon a ladder that leads to nowhere. True ambition may require you to give this comfort up and find another ladder that is worthy of your cause, or to utilize your position on the ladder you are currently climbing to further your cause. That is a tough decision, which we will discuss later.

A Day at the Races

If you have ever seen a greyhound race, you are familiar with the method employed to make the dogs run around the track. A lure, usually an artificial rabbit (or hare if you want to get technical), runs along the inside of the track just ahead of the greyhounds. The dogs chase after the hare and the race ensues. Those in the front of the pack struggle to outpace each other so that they can be the one that captures the lure running ahead of them. While the leaders are competing to catch the lure, the dogs in the rear of the pack may not even see it, but they know that the other dogs are chasing after something and feel compelled to try to get there as well. I think that is very similar to the race that many of us are running in our careers. We are chasing an artificial rabbit—a lure that is just ahead of us and will always be slightly beyond our reach no matter how fast we run.

Some of us are leading the race and far ahead of any competitors, but we ignore this fact and remain focused on that artificial rabbit that we will never catch. Furthermore, if we ever were to catch the rabbit dangling in front of our noses, just image the grief that would overcome us upon the realization that it is not even real. This is similar to the plight of many people who have become "successful" in the eyes of others. From an outsider's perspective, they are winning the race. They are able to run faster, cash in on more winnings, and gain more adoration from the fans. But to the runner, this is not enough. Every time the gate opens and the lure launches off ahead of them, they run as if they have never won a race before. They are no longer running a race against the other competitors; they are struggling in a chase to catch something they have never been able to secure.

Others are running mid-pack, jockeying for position amongst their competitors. This is probably where the majority of the runners are. This is the area where it is easy to get lost in the pack. In addition, it is possibly the most dangerous position because one misstep could lead to a trampling from the other runners. To these runners, catching the lure chased by the leaders may seem to be a somewhat unrealistic goal. Instead of attempting to catch the lure, these runners may simply try to get ahead of the others running mid-pack and make it to the tail-end of the lead pack. Their goal is to chase after other competitors not for the sake of winning the race, but just for the recognition of being in the lead pack.

A lot of us do this at work. We run fiercely and get into a position to fight our way up to that lead pack thinking that we will be satisfied with the status of being a part of the lead pack. What we fail to realize is that the lead pack got to the front because they are running even faster. Now we must maintain a more urgent pace simply to keep from falling behind and dropping back into the obscurity of running mid-pack. With every turn, we must expend more and more energy simply to maintain our status as one of the top dogs.

What are you doing? Are you running around a track as fast as you can under the illusion that once you catch that lure, your race will be complete and you will be satisfied? As long as we base our perception of success on the accomplishment of tasks, such as catching our own metaphorical rabbit, we are blind to the true fulfillment that only comes through relationships and discovering our sense of significance. As long as we are on the earth, our race never really ends. We can retire and live off the savings we have accumulated through the accomplishment of tasks, but this does not constitute true success. It only means that we have quit chasing the rabbit.

As I have stated before, there is nothing wrong with competition. It can bring out the best in us and push us to levels that we never before realized were possible. This is why it is important that we align our efforts with our values and mission. By doing so, we will be able to leverage our competitive nature to further our mission rather than use it for a shot of adrenaline while chasing an artificial lure. By the way, almost every one of us has a competitive nature to some extent. How else could a simple game of Pictionary© with friends generate so much angst and hostility?

Stop to consider the races you are running. What is your lure? Why are you chasing it? With whom are you competing? For most of us, the primary race we are running pertains to our careers, our lure is success, we are chasing it in search of self-validation, and we are mainly competing against ourselves. Once again, we have gotten this all wrong!

First, consider the races we choose to run. An athlete in a track and field competition will not compete in every single race during a weekend's events. To do so would only limit their overall effectiveness. Likewise, we cannot expect to run every race that comes our way in life and perform at a high level in each one. Whenever we run a race, we expend energy and consume resources, thus making it necessary to choose those races that mean the most to us.

Now, let's jump to the question of why we are competing. Whether it is a promotion, a raise, a new house, or a three-legged race at a family reunion, I believe that our main competitive drive stems from the need for self-validation and our primary competitor is ourselves. This is particularly true if the majority of our efforts are concerned with tasks and goals that do not contribute to our mission or fuel our passions. As discussed earlier, we find true fulfillment from following our passions, building relationships, and living a life of significance. In the absence of these things, we look elsewhere for a sense of fulfillment, mainly in the fleeting sense of validation we receive from beating out a competitor for a promotion.

If we have not yet set out on the road to significance, we will lack true self-validation because, intrinsically, we will know we are not fulfilling our mission. Because we lack self-validation, we feel that we are failing in the race and begin to pick up the pace in an effort to gain success and obtain self-validation. Due to the misconception that we can measure success by the amount of money, power, and recognition we have, we turn to the venue that can most reliably provide these rewards—our careers.

Remember that every race we run consumes our resources and may adversely affect our performance in the other races of life. Because we increase our efforts as they pertain to our careers and the search for success, other areas of our life that could actually offer fulfillment and self-validation begin to suffer. The resulting paradox is that we are never able to achieve self-validation or a sense of significance because we exert too much energy being "successful."

So how are we our own biggest competitor? I think those who find true success in life are not necessarily the people who win every race they enter. Those who find true success are the people who chose the right races to enter and then run them to the best of their ability. Everything that you make a priority over your mission will compete against it in terms of your time, effort, and resources. You get to decide where you focus your efforts and which races to run, but without putting your mission first, your mission has to compete against your own errant quest for self-validation through the attainment of success.

At some point, you will realize this and I hope for your sake that you have the courage to do something about it. Believe me—it will take a lot of courage. That is why so many people suffer through their careers and complain endlessly. Of the many reasons we need courage in this situation, a couple of the most obvious are the uncertainty of changing careers and the potential lack of financial security. These are often scapegoats for a greater underlying fear—the fear of stepping away from success as defined by others. Not only do we become accustomed to the material aspects of our false success, but we also grow attached to the identity our false success bestows upon us. Even if we dislike our ladder, we like the fact that most people have to look up from their positions to see the rung on which we are standing.

The Courage to Give Up "Success"

Success breeds success. There is a definite truth to that statement. Once others perceive us as being successful, they expect us to continue to succeed. Because others expect us to succeed, success comes much more easily. Our success originates because of something within us—our drive, competitiveness, skills, knowledge, or perseverance. Moreover, our initial success is generally in an area in which we are more talented and, therefore, of greater interest to us. As we move through life, other people's perception of our success begins to influence us and erode away our internal sense of success that once came from pursuing our passions.

We feel that in order to propagate our success, we have to pursue the careers and the job titles that others expect of us. We deviate from the original nature of our success and move deeper into a world shaped by others. The result is multitudes of people who make a lot of money and have a great deal of power but are completely miserable with their careers. Almost every day, they feel a longing to quit their jobs and do something that interests them—something for which they have a passion. Almost every day, they silence that longing because they want people to continue to perceive them as being successful even if they are miserable with their careers.

Let me be clear on this point. Anyone who relies on the perception of others to shape their career is setting himself or herself up for a lifetime of disappointment. You may believe that you just have to put your dreams and passions on hold until retirement and focus on them at that time. As of the time of this writing, I am not anywhere near the age of retirement, but I know enough about myself to realize that following this thought process would have left me regretting how many years I had wasted not focusing on my mission in life. Choose your ladders and your races wisely, but just as importantly, have the courage to try a different one if the one you have chosen is leading you away from where you need to go.

We have seen this situation portrayed in films and on television. Unfortunately, it happens in real life as well. A professional becomes completely engrossed in their work and the pursuit of success. Their family takes a backseat, personal relationships outside the family are almost nonexistent, and they entirely dismiss a relationship with God. Why is this? The easy answer is that they gave in to greed and material possessions; however, this was not true in my case.

In my own story, I was chasing success. I bought into the false definition of success and was doing everything I could to make more money, have more power, and gain more recognition. I did this not because I wanted more of any of these things; I did this because I wanted more of the success that I mistakenly believed these things represented. I also erroneously believed that this was the right thing to do because it demonstrated ambition, leadership, perseverance, and would lead to a better life for my family.

The promotions and recognition that came with my "success" reinforced my misconception that chasing it was the right thing to do. Other people came to appreciate my success and expected me to continue along the same path. This is the point where I realized I had lost the courage to attempt running a different race. I was in the lead pack of the race I had chosen and closer to that artificial rabbit than I had ever been before, but despite this seemingly successful run, I still lacked fulfillment. In fact, there were times that I absolutely despised the race I was running, but because I lacked the courage to admit that I was in the wrong race, I just kept running.

Why did I keep chasing that rabbit? It was not as if I didn't know that I was running the wrong race. There was no doubt in my mind that I would eventually come to a point in my life where I would change my direction if I could just muster the courage. I knew that other races were probably not as lucrative as the one I was running, but I also knew that my family could live comfortably even if I changed my focus. I had the support of my wife who constantly encouraged me to escape my imprisonment and seek fulfillment rather than success. What was it that kept me from stepping out and choosing a new path? It was my lack of courage and humility to deny my own success.

We first need the courage to believe that our fulfillment comes from doing something significant with our talents and resources rather than from the praise and accolades of others. Even though the success we achieve by pursuing raises and promotions may be false, it is still a boost to our self-esteem to know that other misguided runners admire our ability to run the race. We harbor this unwarranted pride to the point that we actually believe that our quest for false success is admirable and we are champions of success.

Of course, there is that nagging sense that we are running as fast as we can for no reason other than to outrun our competitors, who themselves are also seeking false success. But we usually attempt to ignore that feeling and instead bask in the glory of our victory. If we are to find true success, we must change this mentality. We have to exhibit the courage to shun the shallow, unfulfilling success that others perceive and turn our attention to those areas in our lives where we can make a lasting, meaningful impact. Not everyone will understand this nor will everyone agree with it, but if your desire is to find a sense of significance in your life, it is necessary.

Once we have mustered the courage to turn our focus away from false success and face our potential plummet in the grand organizational chart of society, we need to have the courage to get out of our comfort zone and explore those areas where we can live out our mission. While we may daydream about changing our focus so that we can pursue our passions with sense of bliss and romanticism, there are reasons why we adhere to the search for false success. It is familiar and humans love familiarity. When it comes to false success, we know the path, we know the key people who will help us achieve false success, we know the challenges, and we generally know what we need to do to overcome those challenges.

On the other hand, think about what it will mean for you to climb the ladder that leads you to the fulfillment of your mission and run the race that offers a sense of significance. This can be a very uncomfortable endeavor because it will likely place you in unfamiliar places, using skills you have not yet mastered, and working with people you do not know.

I never said that fulfilling your mission would be easy—if it were, a lot more people would be doing it. In fact, when you consider the courage it takes to give up artificial success, the effort required to reestablish yourself with a new focus, and the magnitude of uncertainty that you will face, fulfilling your mission is sure to be quite difficult. However, you are not reading this book because your current career focus is too difficult, are you? You are reading it because your career focus has left you empty, unfulfilled, and searching for significance. Fulfilling your mission may be difficult, but the labor is sweet and the rewards go far beyond having a big house and a new car.

If you are still having difficulty finding the courage to break free of your imprisonment, consider the alternative. You can choose to continue living a life of cowardly mediocrity while reaping the unfulfilling rewards of false success. You can ignore the emotion that there is more to life and that you are wasting what precious little time you have here on earth. You can also lie to yourself and say that you are making this sacrifice to provide a better life for your family. If you choose this path, then you must accept the fact that you will spend your professional career with an insatiable void due to the absence of significance and fulfillment. Eventually, this emotion will give way to regret as you spend your retirement reflecting on what you could have done had you simply changed your focus.

A Different Race on the Same Track

I want to reinforce that climbing a new ladder or running a different race does not necessarily mean that you have to quit your job and start all over again. Some of you may be in a profession that is an excellent platform for you to further your mission; you just need to change your focus. This may mean taking your professional skills into different arenas where they can benefit others or it may mean turning your workplace into your mission field. Either way, the key is to take your focus away from job titles and income and instead place it on what you need to accomplish in order to fulfill your mission.

This focus depends on your individual talents, passions, and values along with the relationships that you have built in your profession. For an engineer, it could be utilizing your employer to provide a new medical device that enhances the lives of patients. For a manager, it could be creating an environment that emphasizes cooperative learning rather than cutthroat competition. For anyone, it could be building meaningful relationships with others so you can influence them morally and spiritually. We establish some of our largest relational networks through our professions. To use this network only for business or personal gain would be a great waste.

Your professional relational network can be a great field to help you to find your sense of significance. Due to the large number of people that we interact with at work, we are bound to see an individual's or a group's needs from time to time. Even if you stick with the task-oriented, impersonal "just business" world, you will discover a few professional needs that will afford you the opportunity make a difference in that person's or group's life. You could take this a step farther. By building a relationship with other people at work, you will eventually come to know their greatest strengths, biggest fears, and most critical personal needs. Once you have discovered the needs of others, you must figure out how your skills and your personal mission can help that individual. This is what will give you an ongoing sense of fulfillment, not a 10 percent raise and new office furniture.

What happens if you uncover needs that you are not equipped meet? That is not a problem. Remember that as you build meaningful relationships with others, you are not only discovering their needs, but also their greatest strengths and passions. Sometimes your role in the problem-solving process will be nothing more than putting two people together. By doing so, you are actually helping two people—the person with a need gets that need met, and the person who helps them receives a sense of fulfillment by utilizing their skills to help someone else. For some people with vast relational networks, being a "broker of goodwill" is their mission. If you seem gifted at building relationships and have a genuine concern for others, your most important role in your professional life will probably be matching one person's needs with another's passions.

The Issue of Time

Another way to explore your passions without changing jobs is to get involved in some extracurricular activities. Whether it is in a church, local government, or civic organization, I am sure you can find something that will help you pursue your passions. You do not have to look very hard to find a way to utilize your talents and passions to help others. The most common excuse used here is, "But I am so busy with my job and other responsibilities. I don't see how I can 'make time' for additional activities." Here's a news flash, Einstein: You cannot "make time" for anything. You can stretch time by moving near the speed of light, but this is not a viable option for most of us with current fuel costs. Another strategy is to spend your day in a budget review, but studies show that this only *seems* to make time go by more slowly.

You cannot manufacture, purchase, store, or borrow time. Every day of your life consists of twenty-four hours whether you spend it watching television, working at a homeless shelter, writing a business strategy, conquering a nation, doing yard work, or alphabetizing your Star Wars collection (which I have actually done). You can waste your money and feel temporary regret, but you can always go out and make more. Waste your time, however, and you will never be able to regain it. That is why the burden of time wasted is much greater than that of money lost. Likewise, the sense of fulfillment from time well spent is superior to that of money well earned.

I know for me, I feel most content in my efforts when I am physically, spiritually, and/or mentally exhausted, yet somehow energized because I know that I have spent my time well in fulfilling my mission. I think this is true for most of us. However, we must exercise caution not to confuse exhaustion due to the efforts of fulfilling our mission with wearisome busyness. We frequently measure our time management effectiveness simply by how many activities we can cram into a day. We end the day fatigued yet with a sense of pride of how many boxes we checked off our task list.

I am a Type-A, get-as-much-done-as-possible type person. Unchecked boxes on a task list haunt me like tiny poltergeists of inefficiency. Many of you probably have the same type of mentality and can empathize with me. For those of us with this affliction, we simply want to complete tasks, attend functions, and finish projects regardless of their significance or the role they play in fulfilling our mission. Match this with a tendency toward being a perfectionist and you have the recipe for unceasing busyness. Coincidently, you also have the typical blueprint of a successful professional in today's business world...or is that "busyness" world?

The rising stars in most businesses share a few common traits. They are driven, aggressive, eager to accept new responsibilities, and willing to go beyond the call of duty to ensure that they complete projects and tasks on time. They also have an acute attunement to their business and understand the perceived importance of being able to change priorities quickly so that their actions match the directives given from higher up the ladder. The missing ingredient for many professionals (and businesses for that matter) is focus. Focusing our efforts based on our values and our mission is what differentiates significance from busyness. Once again, let's look at what we are taught through our typical experiences at work.

The Unfocused Business

Upon the publishing of the end-of-quarter financial results, you discover that your division has lost more than five million dollars. An investigation of the financial variances reveals that labor inefficiencies were a major contributor to the poor financial performance. In most businesses, the reaction to this type of performance is to get out more production with fewer people. Your division eliminates a significant amount of indirect labor from the budget and places a moratorium on purchases and activities that do not directly contribute to production, such as employee training. In an effort to reduce spending, you place equipment upgrades and even routine maintenance on hold. The message sent to employees is, "We want you to work harder and produce more while your support is reduced and your machines become dilapidated."

After a month or two of severe cost cutting, a new problem emerges. Customer backorders have been steadily climbing and are reaching alarming levels. The new mandate is to crank out as much production as possible with little regard to cost in hopes that the shear volume of production and absorbed overhead will exceed the costs required to increase production. You beef up staffing, allow overtime, and spend money on machine upgrades and maintenance; however, machine downtime to allow for thorough maintenance is unacceptable. The message that now received by employees is, "We want you to produce as much product as possible as fast possible, regardless of the cost."

This operating strategy continues for a while until the next major problem arises. Customer complaints regarding product quality climb to unacceptable levels and internal rejects produce "product-flow constipation." As the company's focus turns to quality, this results in the discovery that the elimination of employee training during the cost-cutting phase to save money remained in effect during the high production phase so that employees could spend their time making product. As a result, you have new employees and individuals who have taken on new responsibilities without receiving the necessary training to allow them to do their job well. Additionally, because of the increased emphasis on production volumes, employees felt pressured to let small defects go in hopes that the customer would not complain. You implement a new training program and reinforce the need to produce a high quality product. Employees now hear, "Get the job done right, even if it means missing a shipping deadline or scrapping a lot of defective product."

This example results in an ongoing roller coaster in which the organization is stuck in a cycle of reacting to problems. The constantly changing priorities and knee-jerk reactions make it difficult for employees to know what is expected of them. This eventually leads to cynicism and a general loss of motivation all because the organization lacks focus.

It may sound like I am beating up on the manufacturing sector, but I just used this example because it is what I know best. The same concept holds true in the service industry, government, and within individuals as well. If you think about it, you are probably not very different from the organization discussed in the example. Whereas that organization had the aspects of operating cost, customer service, and product quality to evaluate, you have various aspects of your life to consider as well. To name a few, we are concerned with our careers, families, personal relationships, spiritual well-being, education, and physical wellness. Without strong values and a resolute mission to guide us, we tend to overreact whenever we perceive a shortfall in one aspect. Just as we saw in the example, this is usually to the detriment of the other aspects in our lives.

Compounding this issue are the ever-growing expectations that we impose upon ourselves (partly a result of our infatuation with entertainment). Our attempt to be all things at all times results in a complete lack of focus in our personal lives. Due to our lack of focus, we hop around from one aspect to another without prioritizing them. Without having priorities and a mission, we cannot understand what we truly desire. Earlier we defined true success as the achievement of something desired; therefore, without focus we cannot have true success.

I am not implying that we should not learn from and adapt to our environment and circumstances. In fact, our ability to adapt plays a key role in discovering true success. However, we should be careful to react only to challenges and shortfalls as they relate to our mission. Too often, we react just for the sake of reacting. If we perceive a problem or shortcoming in our life, we come up with a quick fix to satisfy our desire to take action instead of evaluating how this setback pertains to our overall mission. This attempt to eliminate our problems through sheer busyness is another failed strategy that transcends the business world and our personal lives.

Finally, we need to possess the courage to say "no" to prevent the overwhelming sensation caused by those responsibilities that have nothing to do with our mission. This is what focus is all about. Our society applauds those who take on more responsibility than they can handle. We brag about sixty-hour workweeks and view the ability to get by on four hours of sleep as a badge of honor. If your career demands this of you, then you are shortchanging some of the more important aspects of your life. It is time for you to get some focus and decide where you need to invest your efforts.

Chapter 5–What is the True Definition of Success?

The goal of this book is not to shun people from striving to achieve success, but to help people differentiate between perceived success and true success. It is really quite simple—perceived success is something *seen* by other people while true success is something *felt* by you. Please understand that I am not getting all touchy-feely and telling you that everyone is a winner as long as you give a good effort and believe in yourself. I have seen people put forth tremendous effort without winning. On the other hand, I know people who put forth miniscule effort and hardly ever lose. We have all heard the saying, "It's not whether you win or lose, but how you play the game." Interestingly, we only hear this when we lose. Perhaps we should expand on this concept a little to include not only how we play the game, but also the choice of the game in which we are playing. Many look like winners but feel like losers because they are playing the wrong game. Alternatively, we may be playing the right game; our only problem is that we are in the wrong position.

When I was growing up, I played football. In junior high, I was a linebacker on defense and center on offense. I moved to defensive end my first year of high school. In all of these positions, you are hitting someone on the other team as hard as you can on practically every play. I liked the physicality of the sport and became a respectable player in each of these positions. I wasn't the biggest, strongest, or fastest player by a long shot, but people knew that I wasn't afraid to stick my facemask in them as hard as I could. In addition, I played relatively smart. I knew where I was supposed to be on each play and what to do in most situations, which helped overcome my physical limitations.

During spring training of my sophomore year, our head coach decided that because I played smart, I would make a good quarterback. Our head coach was one of the top coaches in the state (racking up his 300th victory during my senior year), but boy did he miss the boat on this one! Until that March, my efforts as they pertained to the game of football focused on hitting the person on the other team as hard as I possibly could. If you know anything about football, you know that this strategy does not work well in the position of quarterback. I moved in the pocket about as smoothly as eighty-grit sandpaper over a pachyderm with a bad case of shingles. Instead of tight spirals, my passes more closely resembled a catapulted convection oven. I dreaded practice because I knew that I would have to endure another day of trying to fill a position that I simply was not suited to fill. By that fall, my coach moved me back to defensive end (I guess he knew what he was doing after all). Once I was back in this position, I was once again a successful player and found a greater enjoyment in the game of football.

The point of this story is to illustrate that even if we are in the right field and pursuing the right mission, if we are not filling the right role in that field, or if our efforts are unfocused as they pertain to our mission, we will be unsuccessful. The goal of players should be to contribute in a manner that helps their team win games. If the only position I ever played was quarterback, I would have failed not only as a quarterback, but also as a football player and athlete. This is because my measurement of success was no longer helping my team win games, but accurately passing the ball to the receivers. I was actually a successful football player once my coaches looked at the big picture to consider how I could better contribute to the team and moved me back to defensive end. Like a football player in the wrong position, I think many people discover their mission only to meddle with it rather than finding out how they can make the biggest contribution toward fulfillment by playing in the right position all of the time.

I want to expand on the earlier definition of successes being the achievement of something desired. I believe true success is finding your mission in life, working towards the fulfillment of that mission, and leaving a legacy that ensures the furthering of your mission after you are gone. Your mission may not pay a high salary, come with stock options, or require you to wear a suit. Because of this, the majority of people may not view you as being successful as you fulfill your mission. Who cares? We have already seen that our sense of fulfillment does not come from what other people think about us. Grow up and get over the high school mentality that admiration and envy from others will bring you happiness.

Do you remember in *The Matrix* when Neo had the choice of taking the red pill or the blue pill? If he took the blue pill, he would go on believing whatever he wanted to believe—blissfully ignorant of his mission. If he took the red pill, he would enter a world of adventure, danger, and purpose. Imagine that you have a similar choice. Take the blue pill and you can have a job making a six-figure salary with a nice office and other people will view you as being a success. However, you will dislike your job, have little time for your family, and no time or energy left to pursue your true passions—resulting in a never-ending internal struggle. Take the red pill and you can have a job making just enough to pay the bills and while other people may not perceive you as a success, you will pursue your passions and find fulfillment. Which one do you choose?

I think we have two conflicting emotions within us. One tells us to go out and pursue whatever it is that inspires us—to try to make a real difference in the world and to stop wasting our time and energy on the daily activities of our life that may offer financial security but no fulfillment. The other emotion tells us that this sort of behavior is irresponsible and irrational. Besides, we have the warmth and comfort provided by our lifestyle of living the status quo and we think that we should be content with the security and safety that this lifestyle provides for our families and our egos. Why should you do something as foolish as to give this up and step into the unknown?

The reason is simple. Your mission is not to be content with the status quo. It is not to go about your everyday life where days, weeks, months, and years are just blurs of recurring issues with little or no significance to the real you. I guarantee you that if this is your approach, you will wake up one day to the realization that too many years have passed and that you missed too many opportunities during your lifetime. You will realize that you spent the most productive part of your life squandering your talents and knowledge, suffocating your passions, and ignoring the voice telling you that there should be more significance to your life.

False success teaches us that to make something of ourselves requires us to get an education and land a high-paying job with a never-ending parade of promotions and raises. We buy into this grand illusion and pour our souls into it hoping that fulfillment will come because of our success. In the end, all we are doing is imprisoning ourselves deeper within the cell. Because our false view of success leaves us so empty, we seek to fill the emptiness with more success, but it will never be enough. Until we discover and pursue our mission, we will always be yearning for more, we will always be questioning our career and our life, and we will always have an empty chasm right through the middle of us.

Once you discover and surrender to your mission, you will still face the thorns and thistles of adversity, you will still have times of frustration, and you will still go through periods of unhappiness, but you will have the peace of mind of knowing that you are contributing to something greater. You will have the fulfillment that comes only when your daily actions are in alignment with your values. You will gain the inspiration only understood by those committed to their passion. You will feel success from within rather than attempt to portray it outwardly. In essence, you will come to life. What a refreshing way to live amongst the multitude of people who look successful on the outside, but are dead to their passions.

This paradigm shift is the most difficult step in the journey to true success. When we think about quitting our high-paying jobs to pursue our mission, it is easy to see that we will have less money and we will not be able to afford the material possessions to which we have become accustomed. It is easy to think that we will throw away the power and authority that we have worked so hard to establish. It is much more difficult to comprehend that once we pursue our mission, our passion for our work will fill that gaping hole that we previously attempted to fill with possessions, power, and recognition. The ability to influence people with whom we have developed relationships will replace the feeling of power that we once had because of our job title and the recognition it afforded us. Because we fill this void, we will not even miss those things that once served as surrogates for true fulfillment.

Furthermore, if we are doing something we are passionate about then there is a good chance that financial reward will come naturally. This is fine as long as it is not our motivation. Conversely, if we do not obtain great financial rewards, that is fine, too. Our reward is the fulfillment that money alone cannot provide. Where do you think you are more likely to find true fulfillment—on a small fishing boat with a grandfather and grandson or on a party yacht off the coast of Bermuda?

Accountability for Our Time and Talents

As I said before, I believe that we will each be held accountable for what we do with the talents and resources we have been given. Included in the accountability for our resources will be the accountability for our time. Those who seek true success will feel just as busy (if not more so) as those who seek false success. Time will not stand still for you because of the noble cause that you are pursuing. The difference that you will feel is the sense of fulfillment and significance in how you have decided to utilize your time. Who among us has not put in a long day only to come home exhausted and wondering what we really accomplished? As long as you maintain your focus and prioritize your efforts so that you are working toward the furthering of your mission, that discipline will grant you peace with your time management decisions.

The same holds true for your talents, skills, and even relationships. When you begin viewing these resources and relationships as they relate to your mission rather than how they can help you become more successful in the eyes of the world, you open the door to a world of true success that the self-interested prisoners of false success fail to perceive.

I have come across a few individuals in my professional career who only regarded other people for what they could do to help them gain success. These people usually hit a ceiling in their attempt to climb their chosen ladder because there comes a point when others see them for who they really are. The higher they climb, the more exposed they become. These individuals eventually lose the respect of their employees and coworkers and end up stagnant in their careers. They stop growing because they stop leading. The reason they stop leading is simple: You can only lead if you have followers. You will only have followers if you can earn their respect. You will not earn their respect until they know that you genuinely care about them and concentrate on what you can do for them rather than what they can do for you.

Some people have a sufficient amount of charisma to climb their ladder while putting on a magnificent charade that they care for others. They may get higher on the ladder even though their genuine intents are selfish, but true success will evade these people as well. Their houses will never be big enough, their cars will never be new enough, their titles will never be lofty enough, and their paychecks will never be obscenely large enough because their hearts are like leaky buckets. Rather than attending to leaks in the container, they attempt to keep it full by adding more water. Their goal is the appearance of fullness despite the wasted effort placed on filling their hearts with something that will quickly drain away. If we are to be accountable for our time and efforts, then we should hold all of the time and effort that we waste on the pursuit of false success with just as high of a degree of contempt as time and effort engaged in outright misconduct.

Something Larger Than Ourselves

I love sports, especially football. I grew up in Tennessee, so by state law I am a Tennessee Vols fan. At the beginning of every home game in Neyland Stadium, The Pride of the Southland Marching Band comes onto the field and pumps up the crowd with their music and marching. The band then forms a giant letter T and the team comes running through the formation to the roaring of a crowd of more than 100,000 people. During the game, something as seemingly minute as a favorable spotting of the ball can cause the band to strike up "Rocky Top" for the 214th time and the crowd sings along with the same enthusiasm as if it were only 103rd it had been played.

Anyone who has attended a sporting event can tell you that the sense of energy in the stadium, at the track, or in the arena is completely different from what you feel watching a game on television. What causes this wave of enthusiasm and adrenaline? It is not as if we're calling the plays or executing them on field. I think we are swept away by the emotion of being a part of something much larger than ourselves. At that instant, as one of thousands of screaming fans, I am no longer just Jason Barr, an individual. I am a part of the Vol Nation.

Let me preface this by saying that I am engineer, not a psychologist, but I think the reason that we so enjoy being a part of something larger is because we realize the smallness of ourselves. One summer my wife, Sara, and I took a vacation to Glacier National Park in northwest Montana. This is the land known as Big Sky Country. I can tell you that the sky is not the only thing that is big there. The mountains are big, the lakes are big, the trees in the old-growth forests are big, and as I found out at a local diner, the pancakes are huge! The recurring sensation I felt as we hiked through the wilderness was just how small I was in relation to my surroundings. My worries, fears, ambitions, and personal achievements seemed insignificant amongst the grandeur of those majestic mountains.

This was at a time near the beginning of my professional career, but I had already begun to climb my ladder toward what I believed to be success. I remember the perspective I gained as we walked along a ridge on the Highline Trail and I overlooked the vastness of creation. I realized that my personal journey of success might afford me some degree of wealth, power, and recognition, but whatever I could gain for myself was completely inconsequential on the grand scale. These mountains, lakes, and forests would be unaffected by my success. Even the pancakes had more of an effect on me than I did on them.

I am not insinuating that we are helpless individuals who can have no impact on the world. We are all very capable of having a far-reaching significance that goes beyond ourselves as individuals. The catch here is that we will only realize this significance when we stop seeking superficial personal success and become a part of something larger. Once again, this is where we need to comprehend the importance of legacies—both those that we create and those that we join as followers.

You probably did not solely create the legacy that you will leave. You were influenced by several people that you respect and who had missions that you believed were worthy of advancing. These people were the leaders who shaped the way you see the world. You learned from them as well as other followers of them and made some discoveries of your own. The conglomeration of what you learned from others and from your own self-discovery is what gives you your worldview. This worldview will determine the nature of your legacy and it originated in part from the various missions of others.

Eventually, the legacy you leave by fulfilling your mission will influence others who will go on to leave legacies of their own. The legacies they leave will in turn influence others who go on to leave their legacies. You get the idea. The legacy that you leave can influence literally thousands of people because the number of those influenced increases exponentially with each generation of the legacy.

This isn't something that takes centuries to grow either. Imagine that you restore homes for a living. You have experience in home construction and remodeling and love the process. You are passionate about taking a dilapidated property and restoring it to its original beauty. After gaining experience and honing your skills, you become more efficient, develop some great contacts, and seek to make a difference beyond what you can do for paying clients. After some careful consideration, you decide that your mission is to help rebuild homes for victims of fires or natural disasters. You start up a nonprofit organization that utilizes charitable donations, material donations from supply warehouses, and volunteer labor. Since the organization is just starting, we can be conservative and say that during the first five years, you undertake two major projects per year. For each of these projects, we'll estimate that your roster of volunteers is twenty people.

Over the course of ten projects (two per year for five years) with twenty volunteers each, you will have had the opportunity to directly share your passion and your mission with two hundred volunteers. Some of these volunteers will find a passion for this type of work while volunteering for you, and they are likely to continue to volunteer for your cause or to start up their own charity work. Others will see the gratitude in the people that they are helping and sense the significance and fulfillment that it brings and seek ways to use their own profession to help others.

Suppose that once a year, only one volunteer decides to make a long-term commitment to your cause or is fundamentally influenced by your mission, that's five people with whom you are directly leaving a lasting legacy in the span of five years. This does not sound very impressive until you consider the further reaching possibilities of those people passing on your legacy to people you do not even know.

Now let's suppose that once every two years one of those five people directly influenced by you decides to start up their own program for helping people in similar situations by utilizing their profession or talents. They have their own network of contacts and are able to recruit volunteers from a different pool of talent. If they have similar success in getting people to make long-term commitments (one per year) and those people begin to start up their own causes, the number continues to grow exponentially.

To help illustrate how explosive the growth of your legacy can be, we will take the previous assumptions and look at the structure of your legacy as it grows. I know this looks a lot like an organizational chart, but this is the best way I could think of to demonstrate this principle.

After the first year, the chart is simple. You have directly influenced one person and helped transform their life. Excluding yourself, your legacy consists of one person.

During year two, you add another person to the number of people that you have directly influenced and we begin to see the propagation of your legacy by someone else. These people will likely put their unique spin on your mission, because they will have a different set of talents, skills, and passions, but since they are descendents of your legacy there is no denying that the pursuit of their own personal mission is a direct result of your influence. Your legacy has increased by two people and now consists of three people.

During the third year, you add another person to your direct legacy, the person who began their own legacy during year two adds a second person, and one of those people begins their own legacy, creating a third generation. Your legacy has increased by three people and totals six people.

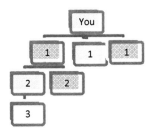

After the fourth year, your legacy grows by five people to a total of eleven. A fourth generation emerges and your legacy grows dramatically.

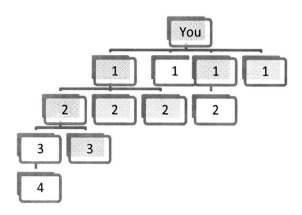

After five years, your legacy increases by eight people to a total of nineteen.

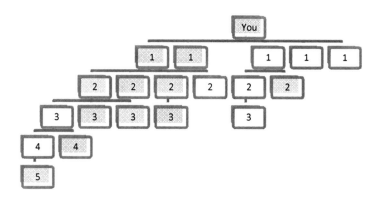

After six years, your legacy increases by thirteen people to thirty-two.

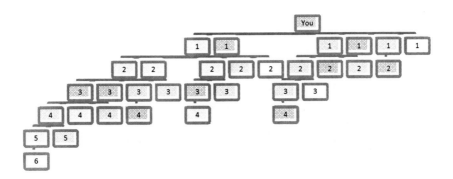

As you can see, even though it may seem your legacy is starting off slowly and you are not having an impact on a lot of people, once you consider how the people you influence will influence others, you can understand how your mission and the values that you instill in others can have a widespread impact. How widespread? The table below shows the number of people added and the total number of people who are a part of your legacy over the course of twenty years.

Year	Additions	Total
1	1	1
2	2	3
3	3	6
4	5	11
5	8	19
6	13	32
7	21	53
8	34	87
9	55	142
10	89	231
11	144	375
12	233	608
13	377	985
14	610	1595
15	987	2582
16	1597	4179
17	2584	6763
18	4181	10,944
19	6765	17,709
20	10,946	28,655

There is actually a mathematical pattern here. Each year, your legacy will increase by the sum of the total of the increase over the previous two years. Yes, you are reading this correctly. Using the assumptions I stated earlier, after twenty years of fulfilling your mission, your legacy will grow to 28,655 people. Granted, many of these people will probably not even know you, but you will have influenced someone who influenced someone who influenced them.

This may seem too good to be true. In order to grow a legacy of almost thirty thousand people in twenty years, all you have to do is add one person to your direct legacy each year and lead others to begin pursuing their own missions and having similar success. The reason this sounds too good to be true is that this is much easier said than done. You will not influence people to change the way they think and to motivate them to further your legacy and start their own legacies with half-hearted speeches, monetary rewards, or even steadfast discipline. This model will only work when you are in tune with your passions and you communicate them through the way you that live. Very few people do this. Most of us go through our lives taking care of our responsibilities, playing it safe, and ignoring our passions. In doing so, we not only deny ourselves true success, but we squander the opportunity have a lasting, positive influence on potentially thousands of people.

Legacies created by individuals who seek to fulfill their missions will result in multiple missions springing from several people who are full of passion. This is in stark contrast to those "legacies" that we often see in the business world. Those are actually nothing more than a leader and a direct band of followers who do little, if anything, to further the legacy by expanding on the mission of their leader. These followers are usually in hot pursuit of false success and seek only the recognition for their efforts, not the furthering of a mission.

We are Transformed by Our Mission

We should seek not to transform the world according to our own selfish desires under the disguise of our mission, but we should allow our mission to transform us. I know this may sound counterintuitive and you are probably asking, "Shouldn't we all be gung-ho and try to make things right in the world?" Yes, we should try to advance our mission toward what we see as being the ideal state, but we also have to be realistic with where the world is right now. I don't mean that we should compromise our mission because the world makes it difficult to pursue or hide our mission because others perceive it as "uncool." When I say we should allow our mission to transform us, I mean we should view the world through our mission's bias and adapt our strategy of dealing with problems accordingly. We may be able to change some aspect of the future of the world, but the way it is at this instant is simply the way it is—we cannot change that. We can argue about the way things are or we can accept the reality of the present and seek to discover the most productive way to engage the brokenness of the world through our mission.

    A common trait of those who pursue false success is that they are constantly trying to change the present state of affairs or they argue with others about what that state is. Some may take this a step further and try to change the past well. This scene plays out around conference tables and dinner tables daily. Rather than being accountable for the current conditions—whether they are production numbers, management decisions, or our life focus—we manipulate data, financial reports, and personal missions to create a fantasyland of fallacies that do absolutely nothing to improve the future. Why do we do this? Because in our hearts, our concern is not with any particular mission or passion, rather, our concern is with positioning ourselves so that we look good no matter the true state of affairs surrounding us. We seek to change the way things *look* because we are too stubborn and prideful to accept the way they *are*. Instead of focusing on the actual situation, we tend to focus on how others perceive us in relation to the situation. When we do this, we put our pride, ambition, and egos above our mission. In other words, we transform our mission for our own perceived benefit rather than letting our mission change us.

I believe this stubbornness is born out of not only our ego, but also our apathy. If we are genuinely concerned with our work—if we are following our passions, then we should be adamant about discovering the truth so that we may be able to make the necessary changes that will bring about real improvements. Our lack of concern for gaining a true understanding of our problems and our attempts merely to change the way things look is a clear indicator that we are not living out our mission.

On the other hand, if we surrender to our mission and have the humility to admit failure, ask for help, and/or change our direction, then we are placing our mission above our ego. Furthermore, when we are fully committed to our mission, it will change the way we see the world. We will no longer think about how a particular event will shape other people's perception of us, but how that event relates to our mission. Remember, we are not only accountable for the things that we do. We are also accountable for the things that we know we should do, but refuse to act upon. Some of the greatest advances are made when leaders have the courage and humility to take their heads out of the sand, accept the disconnect between the way things are and the way things could be, and allow themselves to be transformed in order for their mission to better engage the world as it currently exists.

Chapter 6–Discovering Your Mission

What is your mission? If you are like most people, you probably don't have the slightest idea. For many, the whole concept of having a personal mission sounds like something from a corny inspirational speech given by a person in a polyester suit with a comb-over. The reason we do not give much credence to the idea of having a personal mission is that our true passion has long ago died. We no longer put much thought into what we really want get out of life or contribute to it and instead rely on other people to tell us what we want to look like, what kind of house we want, what kind of education we want, and in the end, what kind of life we want. We are all living for something—you can take the time to decide for yourself what your purpose is or you can let someone else tell you. Too many of us are letting someone else dictate our lives because we lack the clarity and courage to seek out and fulfill our own personal mission.

Understanding your personal mission is not just something that is nice to do once a year or at a leadership conference, it is an ongoing necessity for you to lead a truly successful life. If we fail to assess where we are focusing our efforts and how those efforts relate to our mission on a regular basis, it will be easy to fall back into the trap of living for the false success that others impose upon us.

How you go about finding your personal mission is up to you. Everyone is different, so to suggest that there is a worksheet you can fill out that will neatly explain why you are here and what you should do with your life would be foolish and contrary to everything that you have read up to this point. The guidelines below are just that—guidelines. Some of these will help, some will not, and some will probably give you ideas for other methods to employ. The important thing here is that you take the time to really understand yourself and shut out all of the noise of the world while you are making the discovery.

Listen to Yourself

Deep down, you know yourself fairly well. The problem is that we often close our minds to ourselves in order to listen to what others want us to be. Society places pressure on us to go into a certain field and follow a specific career path in order to be successful. This is great if your heart is truly in your career, but what do you do if there is a nagging voice that regularly reminds you that what you are doing is not the right path for you?

Throughout much of my career in manufacturing, I heard this voice. I grew up tinkering with things. I liked to build models, take things apart to see how they worked (usually unable to put them back together, to my parent's dismay), and I was talented in math and science. A logical career choice for me was engineering. I went to college, got a degree in mechanical engineering and joined the job force. My first job was as a manufacturing engineer in an industrial facility. I never fully appreciated my love for the outdoors until I started spending fifty to sixty hours a week inside a building with few windows and a lot of noisy machinery. In the winter, it was possible to go an entire workweek without ever seeing the light of day. There was a voice telling me, "This isn't right. You will never by happy in this environment."

At the time, I was still under the influence of false success. My response to this voice was, "I'm not going to listen to you. Work is about diligence, perseverance, and making sacrifices. Besides, look at how much money I'm making and what I can buy with it. It is more than enough to justify my unhappiness." I ignored my feelings so I could continue plugging away at what I felt was the responsible, logical career path that would lead me to success.

After a very short period of having the word "engineer" in my title, I got into management. Promotions came along with various relocations. I was moving halfway across the country at the rate of about once every two years. By the time I was thirty-one years old, I had lived in seven different states in eight years. Early in my career, these moves were exciting and seemed like an adventure, but once Sara and I had our first child, the voice was back. I knew that our child would need more stability than the nomadic lifestyle we were leading could offer. Furthermore, I knew that the stress and time commitments of my career were taking away from my effectiveness as a father and a husband. The voice was getting louder.

Over the years, I attempted to ignore the voice. I considered it unhealthy doubt and was willing to silence it in order to pursue the next step in my career. I thought that to listen to it—to give up my career and success in order to pursue my desires—would be selfish and irresponsible. It was not until the voice came to represent something more than myself that I began to listen to it. This voice was no longer a ghost of my doubts; it was desperate plea for the welfare of my child. It was my conscience. It was God speaking to me. It was a voice of reason from beyond the frantic world of self-indulgent success.

I finally realized that it was not selfish to listen to this voice; it was selfish it ignore it. The reason I refused to listen to that voice was because I wanted to continue to live a life in which others would think I was successful. I was addicted to success and the continual validation it offered me. Whenever I felt frustrated, all I had to do was think about how far I had gone in my career in such a short time. My career success had become a psychological crutch on which I supported all of the fears and doubts surrounding my career choice.

My encounters with professionals in various fields confirm that many of us deal with this internal struggle on a regular basis. We have the disparaging feeling that what we are doing with our lives is not right. We are frustrated with our work environment, office politics, or the shear nature of our work. Our inner voice tells us that it's just not worth it anymore and we need to get out. Then we get a raise or a promotion and fall back into the masquerade of success that silences our conscience.

Every time we ignore ourselves and follow the path of false success, we kill ourselves a little more—becoming more and more dead to the wonders of what our lives could be if we pursued our passions. Each promotion and each raise serves to entrench us deeper. Our conscience knows this, so it has to call out more loudly and more urgently. That promotion that we thought would give us fulfillment actually widens the disparity between who we are and who we want to be. In fact, the daily frustrations of work did not bother me as much as the internal struggle between what I wanted to do with my life and the numbness that false success created in it.

As I stated earlier, I am a Christian and I believe the voice of our conscience is also the voice of God. Whether you believe this or not, I am certain there is a voice that guides your decisions. I strongly urge you stop ignoring it. You will never reach your fullest potential by ignoring your conscience. You will only become more of something that you do not inwardly desire to be. People may think of you as being successful, but you will be nothing more than an imposter—a confused individual who regards the perception of others more highly than your own passions. This is a sign of cowardice, laziness, and resignation.

Read Ecclesiastes

Regardless of your religious background and beliefs, the book of Ecclesiastes in the Bible can offer you some great insight to the role your career plays in your life. This philosophical book reads like poetry and is full of wisdom. It is a relatively short book and you can read it in one sitting. The following are a few highlights.

Simple pleasures are meaningless (chapter 2, verses 10 and 11).

> I denied myself nothing my eyes desired;
> I refused my heart no pleasure.
> My heart took delight in all my work,
> and this was the reward for all my labor.
> Yet when I surveyed all that my hands had done
> and what I had toiled to achieve,
> everything was meaningless, a chasing after the wind;
> nothing was gained under the sun.

It is remarkable how relevant an Old Testament book written thousands of years ago is to our working world today. We have an emptiness inside us that we can only fill by pursuing our mission. Rather than pursue our mission, we try to fill this emptiness with possessions and pleasures. These possessions and pleasures require money. Since our careers are our source of income, we view them as the vehicles that will bring us those possessions and pleasures that will fill our emptiness. However, just as the writer (known as The Teacher) tells us in Ecclesiastes, this void will never be filled by that which we can buy. We fool ourselves into believing that since we were unable fill the void, the possessions and pleasures we had attained were not enough. Therefore, we strive to make more money so we can afford more expensive possessions and pleasures while getting further away from the thing that will bring us true fulfillment. The book expresses a similar concept later on. "And I saw that all labor and all achievement spring from a man's envy of his neighbor. This too is meaningless, a chasing after the wind" (Ecclesiastes 4:4).

Toil is meaningless (Ecclesiastes 2: 17-23).

> So I hated life, because the work that is done under the sun was grievous to me. All of it is meaningless, a chasing after the wind. I hated all the things I had toiled for under the sun, because I must leave them to the one who comes after me. And who knows whether he will be a wise man or a fool? Yet he will have control over all the work into which I have poured my effort and skill under the sun. This too is meaningless. So my heart began to despair over all my toilsome labor under the sun. For a man may do his work with wisdom, knowledge, and skill, and then he must leave all he owns to someone who has not worked for it. This too is meaningless and a great misfortune. What does a man get for all the toil and anxious striving with which he labors under the sun? All his days his work is pain and grief; even at night his mind does not rest. This too is meaningless.

Talk about a downer! Upon first reading this, you may think that the writer is suffering from some serious manic depression. It sounds as if he has thrown in the towel and given up hope for any meaning in life, but look at the passage again. He is not saying life is meaningless nor is he saying that a person's work is meaningless. He is saying that *toil* is meaningless.

Toil is more than just labor. Toil is exhaustive, wearisome, painful labor. Any kind of labor can become wearisome over time, but I think here the writer is referring to work done that is not in alignment with our values and passions. The toil of which the writer is speaking is not physically exhaustive but emotionally exhaustive and this emotional exhaustion comes from an inner struggle between the person we have allowed ourselves to become and our true self.

Relationships are more important than achievement (Ecclesiastes 4:7-12).

>Again I saw something meaningless under the sun:
>There was a man all alone;
>he had neither son nor brother.
>There was no end to his toil,
>yet his eyes were not content with his wealth.
>"For whom am I toiling," he asked,
>"and why am I depriving myself of enjoyment?"
>This too is meaningless –
>a miserable business!
>Two are better than one,
>because they have a good return for their work:
>If one falls down,

his friend can help him up.
But pity the man who falls
and has no one to help him up!
Also, if two lie down together, they will keep warm.
But how can one keep warm alone?
Though one may be overpowered,
two can defend themselves.
A cord of three strands is not quickly broken.

You have seen this story portrayed in countless movies, books, and in real life. Whether it is Buddy's dad in the movie *Elf* or Bob from the house at the corner, the concept is essentially the same as that written in Ecclesiastes—if you ignore your personal relationships to seek wealth and glory, true success and happiness will evade you. The reason this is a popular storyline is because we know it to be true and we struggle with it regularly. It is so simple when we see the story from a third-person perspective. In these cases, it is obvious to us that the characters need to step away from their pursuit of glory and spend some time with their family. Yet when we face the same decision in our own lives, the water becomes murky and we often choose work over relationships. We justify our actions by convincing ourselves that our situation is different and we are concentrating on work so our family will benefit, but our families and friends don't need more of what we can buy for them, they need more of us.

There are many more lessons that you can learn from reading Ecclesiastes and I encourage you to do so. Even if you have never opened a Bible in your life, you can glean much wisdom from reading it and reflecting on how it applies to your personal struggles.

Go Back to Childhood

The dreams of your youth can provide some wonderful insights to what you really want to do with your life. Those early years of our life are all about discovery, hope, and anticipation. Children have grand ideas and big imaginations when it comes to what they want to be when they grow up. Their inner voice and outward expressions are one in the same because they have not yet turned away from their passions and have endless possibilities. They have yet to deviate from who they truly are in order to follow the career path that leads to security and success. They have not yet surrendered to the expectations of their society.

Spend some time with children talking to them about what kind of job they want to have when they are out on their own and you will quickly find that they have the whole concept of fulfillment mastered. They don't say that they want to be a middle manager because of the financial stability and security such a profession can provide. They have aspirations such as being an astronaut, a major league ballplayer, or an archeologist. They desire to do the things that capture their wonder and passion. Does your job capture your wonder and passion? If not, then is it not obvious why you are so eager to find something that will?

I fully appreciate the fact that life imposes more than a few limitations on us as we approach adulthood. I realize that we cannot all be lollipop tasters, professional kickball players, or video game critics when we grow up. However, we can think back to those things that inspired us in our youth—those activities that opened our eyes in wonder—and find a way to fit them into our personal mission. It just takes a little creativity. You still have some of that left, don't you?

Here is an example. My dad always loved music. He would come home for lunch, put on those great big Howard Cosell headphones, and soak it in. If he had any musical talent whatsoever, he would have played an instrument or sung at every opportunity. His only problem was that he had no talent when it came to making music. This is similar to the scenario many of us face. He had a passion (music) and he had a limitation (the inability to make music). In situations such as this, we can throw our hands in the air claiming that there is no way for us to pursue our passions, or we can use our creativity to discover an alternate method to pursue our passions.

While my dad could not make music, he had a very good ear for how it should sound. He was also a techie and loved electronics. His solution was to volunteer as the sound technician at our church and he did so very well. He became a part of something that he was passionate about despite a lack of talent and skills directly related to that area. He did this by focusing on what he could do well and linking that to his passions rather than resigning to his limitations.

We can take the same approach as we discover our mission. Go back and rediscover your passions, accept your limitations, and find ways to apply your talents. That application may not be conventional or glamorous, but it sure beats sleepwalking through our careers as we cling to a life of dispassionate advancement. The fusion of our passions and talents make for a formidable force that will lead to true success.

Go Forward to the End

Another exercise to consider when discovering your mission is looking forward to your own end. How do want others to remember you? What do you want people to say about you at your funeral? What stories do you want to pass on to your great-great grandchildren? What lasting impact do you want to have on the lives of others? Take some time to give this some thought and write down your ideas.

Your list will probably include some ambitious statements that are intimidating at first glance. Your next step is to take these ambitious statements and break them down into incremental goals. The lifetime achievement of starting a family business to pass down through the generations may seem daunting, but the individual steps of performing market research, writing a business plan, raising capital, acquiring a place of business, and executing the business plan are achievable. Breaking down long-range achievements into short-range goals is very simple and nothing more than common sense, but we rarely do it effectively.

Whatever your long-range goals, it is vitally important that you understand how you want to contribute to the lives of others because this is how you will ultimately be remembered.

This is your identity. Because we focus on how others perceive our current level of success, we mistakenly think that our identification comes from our careers and professional achievements. We spin our wheels in the mire of false success so others can admire our work. In the end, people do not really care what we have achieved. They will remember us by how we influenced them and how we made them feel. What are you doing today to influence the lives of others? How do people feel after being in your presence? These are important, yet often-overlooked components of your mission as you seek true success.

By our nature, we are relational beings—we want others to share in our happiness, sadness, joy, and pain. I think we achieve the highest level of fulfillment by pursuing our passions, applying our talents, and having people truly appreciate our work. However, we need to be careful not to confuse the appreciation of true success with the recognition of false success. The recognition of false success is the notice others take of our work only for its merit as work. Do you remember the example from Chapter 1? When Ima Realperson is recognized for her documentation system that tracks changes to the documentation system that controls the approval system that allows changes to documents, it is recognized simply as a piece of work. There is no personal appreciation for her accomplishments, merely a superficial acknowledgement of effort.

True success comes from something deeper. Because we are relational, I believe we will rarely feel truly successful in what we do without the heartfelt appreciation of others. This appreciation is much deeper than the temporary pride we feel when someone says we did a good job or gives us a promotion because we "have a good track record." This appreciation comes from people whose lives have changed because of what we do, what we believe, and how we live.

Overcome Your Need to be an Expert

Another obstacle that we face as we consider the prospect of taking on a new endeavor is our lack of mastery in that field. We have a level of expertise in our careers that affords us a certain degree of comfort that we obliterate by venturing out into a less familiar field. Throughout our careers, we work hard to educate ourselves, obtain specific experience, and gain credibility that is specific to our work. While expertise can be a great asset, it can also be a significant barrier.

During my years in manufacturing, I saw quite a few people leave the various facilities where I worked in order to take on new jobs. The majority of the people who moved on not only remained in manufacturing, but they took jobs in facilities that manufactured the same products. Because of this, their new jobs were very similar to the ones that they were leaving. I can understand that having knowledge and experience in a specific area increases your marketability within it, but I cannot understand the thought process behind some of these people. They complained endlessly about the various aspects of their careers from corporate politics to regulatory agencies, but when they finally summoned the courage to leave their jobs, they jumped right back into the same old problems with different companies. They were happy for the first few weeks, but as soon as the honeymoon ended, the same complaints would begin to surface.

The only conclusion I can draw from this behavior is that we prefer that which we dislike because it is more familiar than the unknown. In other words, we would rather be disgruntled experts than hopeful novices. Once again, I think it all goes back to self-esteem and our need to fuel it through the positive perception of others. Our desire for professional success requires that we be self-sufficient experts. We feel that the only place for novices is in the entry-level positions filled by recent college graduates seeking to gain experience. Likewise, we view a lack of expertise by a tenured employee as a sign of professional weakness. The fear of showing any vulnerability in our armor of expertise results in the "fake it 'til you make it" mentality on which some people base their careers.

As I have said before, humility is one of the key components that will allow you to find true success. If you surrender to your mission and allow it to transform you, it will take you to places you have never been and require you to explore new fields in which you lack expertise. This is the stopping point for many would-be truly successful individuals because they lack the courage to expose themselves to a new field, preferring instead to cling to their accomplishments that reside in the past. These people are like the thirty-something-year-old ex-high school football player who still lives in the past reminiscing of his glory days. His best days are in the past because he clings to that bit of success that he once experienced.

It's fine to remember our past, but we are mistaken if we think we can rely on our past successes to bring ongoing fulfillment. In the same manner, we cannot rely solely on our expertise to bring us true success. Achieving true success and fulfilling our mission requires us to humble ourselves so that we can open our eyes to the possibilities that are beyond our expertise. In fact, I believe that if you periodically are not completely at a loss of direction, then you are not letting your mission take you far enough. Instead, you are relying on your expertise and riding comfortably on the Status Quo Express.

As you take this ride, you may look out your window and occasionally see others who are struggling as they attempt to find their own direction. Your first response may be to smirk smugly as you witness their struggle; then that annoying voice comes back and beckons you to pursue your own passions. Your next emotion is envy as you admire the plight of those who are not on the train because you realize that they are not passengers. They are sojourns who temporarily struggle as they live a life of adventure and fulfillment while advancing their mission.

"But my job is demanding, not just a first-class train ride," you say. I am not challenging the difficulty of your job or the roadblocks that you must overcome regularly. I am challenging which roadblocks you allow yourself to tackle because of the road you choose. Think of it like lifting weights. We all know that if you lift weights regularly, you will gain muscle. However, if you do the same exercises in the exact same manner, your body will adapt to the challenge and you will eventually reach a plateau in which you are no longer building muscle but sustaining the muscle already built when you overcame past challenges. You will still sweat when you exercise. You will still have to put forth effort and you will feel fatigued afterward, but you will no longer be growing.

The only way to get past this plateau and build more muscle is to change up your exercise regimen. You have to use a heavier weight, change up the number of repetitions and sets, or work out the muscles using different exercises. You have to do new things that challenge your muscles in new ways. This sounds basic when put into physiological terms, but many of us are stuck in the same rut in our professional lives. We keep doing the same routine, yet we cannot understand why we lack growth and fulfillment. I think the main reason we keep doing the same things in our professional lives is that we desire the comfort provided by our expertise in those areas of familiarity. Our reliance on expertise is in proportion to our lack of courage and our need to appear successful despite our lack of growth. Unfortunately, many of us are content to sit on this plateau throughout our professional lives.

The intent of this chapter is not to be an exhaustive guide on how to find your mission. I just want to give you some ideas and let you know what helped me. Many authors have already done a much better job with the subject of actually discovering your mission. In particular, I suggest that you read *Wild at Heart*, by John Eldredge, and *Purpose Driven Life*, by Rick Warren. Even better, find someone else to read these with you and discuss the books as you read them. Whatever you do, I strongly encourage you to take the next step. The goal of this book is to get you to think, but thought without action is like a seed without water. It has the potential to grow into something much larger and productive, but without that extra ingredient, it will remain small and unchanged.

Chapter 7–The Brave Few

So far, we have seen that success as defined by others does not match our own definition of success. We pour ourselves into seeking false success and we dedicate most of our time and effort to it while leaving little to seek out and fulfill our mission. This creates an internal struggle that leads to a lack of fulfillment and unhappiness with our careers. We feel our lives should have greater meaning than to be cogs in the machine and we search for ways to add significance to our careers. Many of us have fleeting visions of what our lives could be while still toiling away in the quest for success. We intuitively know what we should be doing and just need to take the time to clarify our mission. Now comes the most difficult part—acting on our convictions.

This is the point where I stalled out for many years. Trapped in my cell of self-imprisonment, I held the key in my hand and I knew the way out, but I just sat there and stared at the door. This is similar to the phenomenon of institutionalization experienced by actual prisoners. In *The Shawshank Redemption*, the character Brooks Hatlen depicted this concept. Brooks spent several years in prison where he made friends, learned a routine, and formed his identity. Although imprisoned, he was comfortable with his surroundings, the predictability of prison life, and the comfort of knowing that as long as he was in prison, he had his identity. Does this sound familiar to any of you? After his release, Brooks had difficulty adjusting to life "on the outside." He struggled with how the world changed and missed his friends in prison—which he referred to as "home." Shortly after his release from prison, the struggle became unbearable and Brooks committed suicide.

I realize this is an extreme illustration, but it is similar to what many of us feel in our careers. After years of living in the comfort of our jobs and the reassurance of our false view of success, we undergo a sort of institutionalization. We no longer know how to live as free people. We may say that we want to get out of our careers and pursue our passions, but our actions reveal that we are content to stay where we are. We have a long list of excuses for not taking the leap, at the top of which is the financial security of our present jobs and the need to provide for our families, but I think the true reason for our hesitation runs deeper. We are afraid of giving up our identities in the world of false success.

We often have our identity bestowed upon us rather than carving it out ourselves. Think about how important a first impression is. An individual may have a heart of gold and a long list of accomplishments, but we remember him as the guy with a cold, limp handshake. Likewise, many of us develop our identities by how others perceive us. In the case of the dead fish handshake, this perception is negative, but what happens if the perception is positive? What if you have a shining success story early in your career that sets you up for the impression of continued success whether there is anything to substantiate it or not?

When we join the working world, we are eager to make a positive first impression. We watch those around us, observing which actions are worthy of reward and seek to emulate them in our careers. At this stage, we are rarely acting on our values or our mission because we are so eager to please others according to their perception of success. As it turns out, the standards for success in our society are relatively low. It is not that difficult to hit a few homeruns early in the game, thereby ensuring future pay raises, promotions, and recognition. I am sure you can identify a few people who have achieved "success" in their careers but are completely void of wisdom, leadership qualities, and any genuine concern for their role in the lives of others. Because we are rewarded based on such superficial expectations, the concept of false success is reinforced.

You are probably familiar with Ivan Pavlov's experiment with canines. Pavlov was a Russian psychologist and physiologist who pioneered the study of what he called "conditional reflexes." He studied dogs by ringing a metronome when he gave them food. Pavlov repeated this process for several days and eventually the dogs began to associate the ringing of the metronome with food and salivated at the sound of it. Pavlov also discovered that the dogs would salivate when they heard the metronome even in the absence of food.

Like Pavlov's dogs salivating at the sound of a bell, we are motivated by those things that have come to represent success—even if they have no substance and provide no true nourishment. If we allow them, they will not only motivate us, they will become our identity. We become Bob the Budget Guru, Connie the Cost Reduction Queen, or Tommy the Terminator. Those personas may not be our true selves, but they are the identity that got us to where we are, and as a result we are reluctant to turn away from them. Those identities have proven to be successful and we are afraid that if we turn from them to pursue our passions, our new identities will not command the perception of success and acceptance by others.

This is why relentlessly pursuing our passions requires a tremendous amount of courage. Not only are we risking our financial security, our steady stream of promotions, and our positional authority, but we are jeopardizing our identity. We fear that the perception of our new (and true) identity will not be as positive as that of our false self. Instead of surrendering to our passions, we let our fears control us and we continue to pursue the world of false success because of its familiarity and the identity we have created within it. I wish I could encourage you by saying that all you must do is follow your dreams and you will succeed, but we all know that the world is not that simple. I can assure you of this—as long as you neglect your passions and live a life based on the pursuit of false success, you will never achieve true fulfillment. You may be content to proceed through the remainder of your life in a big home with a nice car while building an impressive retirement fund, but this will be of little consolation while searching for your own sense of significance.

So how do you give up this false identity and seek significance? Once again, everyone is different and there is no checklist to prepare you for that step. The points that follow are some of the things that helped me take the leap. They may or may not work for you, but I encourage you to put some thought into how you will come to terms with the fact that giving up on false success will change your identity. It will change the way people perceive you and the way you think. It is important to understand your mission and it is vital to have the courage to step out and pursue it, but it is also important that you prepare yourself mentally before taking this step.

Ensure that Your Mission Means More to You than False Success

The pursuit of your passions may end up being a financially rewarding endeavor that provides you with all of the material comforts and prestige you enjoyed in the world of false success. Alternatively, the pursuit of your passions may leave you struggling to meet your budget and you may lack recognition from your peers. Either way, you must maintain your perspective.

By the time you are ready to step out and pursue your passions, you should have already spent a significant amount of time considering some of the following questions:

- What is of the most importance to you?

- What are your greatest skills and talents?
- How can your skills and talents benefit others?
- What do you want to achieve through your work?
- With whom will you interact in the pursuit of your mission?
- How do you want to influence others?
- What impact do you want to have in your chosen mission field?
- What will you sacrifice in order to pursue you mission?
- What uncompromising values will you uphold in the pursuit of your mission?
- What left you unfulfilled in the world of false success?

Answering the questions above will help you understand why your mission is important to you and will offer clarification in times of turmoil. I recommend that you spend some time giving the questions careful consideration and make a list of additional questions and answers you feel may offer you some guidance down the road. After you have done this, write a brief mission statement describing your mission and your priorities. If you have never undertaken this endeavor, you probably think that writing a personal mission statement is, well, dorky. It is a shame that in our world today, many companies, organizations, and clubs have mission statements, while the people who comprise them frantically run around trying fulfill all of their obligations without a clue as to what their own personal mission statement looks like. We seem to think that as long as we're busy doing something, we are being productive and contributing to our society.

The purpose of this mission statement is to provide you with the framework for true success. If you run into a difficult situation or feel you are digressing from your purpose, pull out your mission statement so that you can chart your position. This will also come in handy when you feel you are failing because of the influence of false success. It is easy to become frustrated when you are struggling to fulfill your mission while others are cruising through raises, promotions, and new houses. In those times, you will need to remember the importance of your mission and that true success is unique to each individual. An eloquent desire for making more money is probably not your heartfelt mission statement. Concentrate on the things you really want to achieve and have faith that the accomplishment of those things will ultimately give you more fulfillment than the rewards of false success.

If the pressure to cave in to false success overwhelms your desire to pursue your mission, then guess what—you have not yet found your mission. You need to go back to square one and figure out your purpose. Perhaps your false success still influenced you during your attempts to discover your mission. Surrendering to your mission means complete and total surrender. If you attempt to cling to any remnant of false success, you will limit the level of significance that you can attain. This is because any hesitation to give up false success is evidence of your lack of commitment.

This was a tough one for me after I left my job to embark on a new journey. I left a high-paying, somewhat prestigious job with a bright future because I knew that something wasn't right. I had certain frustrations that were a product of my work environment (politics, annoying coworkers, high stress, etc.), but my biggest reason for leaving was the lack of fulfillment in what I did every day. I wanted to do something more productive with my time and talents than sitting in a conference room listening to the same old arguments by the same people. I wanted to be able focus my efforts on the things that could actually make a difference in the lives of others rather than hastily put out as many fires as possible so that someone, somewhere, could check a box off their "to do" list. I wanted to dedicate my time and energy to the things that I considered of most importance to me.

Immediately after leaving my job, I felt a great sense of relief. My wife took a new job and we moved to Georgia. The plan was for me to spend some time trying to figure out what my next step was while taking care of our daughter who was seven months old at the time. Talk about a humbling experience! I went from being a young hotshot manager on the fast track in a very powerful company to Mr. Mom overnight. There were some similarities (soothing someone to make them stop crying, cleaning up messes while new ones were being created, and dealing with a lot of, well, crap), but for the most part, my daily responsibilities changed drastically.

My wife had some concerns about this change for me. She knew how seriously I took my job and how hard I had worked to get to where I was, but I can honestly tell you that I have never regretted my decision and I doubt that I ever will. By stepping out on a leap of faith, I was able to become a much greater part my daughter's life. I was able to find a purpose that went far beyond bonuses and stock options. I no longer had to be the dad that left for work before anyone else in the house was awake and came home only to spend one or two exhausted, stress-filled hours with my family before bedtime. I pity those who miss the opportunity to be a genuine presence in their child's life because they are too busy building a career that they mistakenly believe will give their family a "better life."

Despite the fact that I was content with my decision to leave Corporate America and to refocus on my family, I was a little uncomfortable with giving up my identity. Because we moved to a new state, we met many new people. Invariably as the introductory conversation turned to the "what do you do for a living" question, I felt compelled to give my life story so that new acquaintances would know that I had not been a househusband all my life. Even after coming to my revelation and throwing away false success, I still needed appreciation of my past success.

Over the next few weeks, I contemplated what my new career was going to be. I had a few guidelines that were legitimate. My new career had to be something I enjoyed, something that would allow me to remain a fixture in my daughter's life by being flexible enough to allow me to work from home at least part of the time, and I wanted to go into business for myself. I also had an additional guideline that I kept to myself—I wanted to be wildly successful in terms of monetary reward and recognition so that I would still be able to cling to my worldly successful identity.

Had I not learned anything? Here I was with a blank canvas and a world of opportunity to pursue my passions yet I was still limiting myself to the areas that I felt would command the respect and admiration of others. I thought I had recovered, but I was having a "success relapse." Fortunately, there is a cure for this affliction. That cure is discovering your mission—the reason why God put you on this earth and gave you the talents and values that He gave you. This is the same reason why you cannot silence that voice that tells you that there is something more even though you may have reached a high level of "success."

While it is essential to ensure that your mission is more important than false success through the lean times, this is equally—if not more important—during times of bounty. This is where many entrepreneurs and would-be mission workers go astray. These people begin by pursuing their passions and get a taste of false success along with true fulfillment. They get to do something they are passionate about, use their talents, help others, *and* accumulate wealth, power, and recognition. This may seem like the best of both worlds, but it is a very slippery slope. These individuals may find themselves beginning to focus more on financial rewards, political power, and public recognition and less on their mission. If this goes unchecked, these people can easily imprison themselves in false success while operating under the veil of pursuing their mission.

This does not mean that you are to shun wealth and recognition as you pursue your mission—just don't make them your primary goals. Figure out what your mission is, set your goals accordingly, and put wealth and recognition in the proper prospective. Wealth and recognition are possible *results* of the fulfillment of your mission, but they should never be the *objective* of your mission.

Earlier, I stated that we all have a mission. Some of us have exercised enough self-leadership to take the time to discover or at least contemplate that mission. Others have surrendered to the societal standby mission of the pursuit of false success. This universal mission places its emphasis on achievement, advancement, wealth, and ego. For years, I was dedicating myself to this mission without even knowing it. I wasn't incredibly materialistic or power-hungry, but I wanted to succeed. I thought that success was a sign of a winner and the result of the efforts of a person dedicated to excellence. I believed success to be a noble goal. Now I know that the race you choose is a far better indicator of your character than how fast you can run.

If you have attained "success" and still lack fulfillment or if you have attempted to follow your heart into a new career only to fall back into the prison of success, then I submit to you that you have never actually linked your passions with your mission. You may have taken a pay cut or passed on a promotion, but you never fully surrendered to your mission. Complete surrender to your mission takes a lot of courage and faith. Courage and faith are endangered qualities in a culture whose recipe for success looks something like this:

Dry and Crumbly False Success

Ingredients
- Proper education
- One eager human
- 1-2 Tbsp each ambition and desire
- 1-5 major corporations
- ¼ tsp wisdom
- 4 Tbsp cynicism
- One 12-oz. can of numbness
- All available buzzwords
- Frequent namedropping
- Raises and promotions to taste

Directions
1. Place one fresh eager human in a quality learning institution and sauté over medium heat for 4-8 years, stirring occasionally.
2. Just before removing the sautéed human, add ambition and desire.
3. In a separate bowl, mix one major corporation with the sautéed human and bake at 450 degrees for 1-3 years.
4. Separate human from major corporation. Squeeze any remaining passion from the human and discard.
5. Add ¼ tsp wisdom and 4 Tbsp cynicism to human.
6. In a separate bowl, stir together remaining major corporations until thoroughly mixed.
7. Chop up dispassionate human and mix with the remaining major corporations. Add the 12-oz. can of numbness, all available buzzwords, and frequent namedropping and bake at 350 degrees for 30-35 years.
8. Baste occasionally with raises and promotions.
9. Test 401(k) for doneness.
10. When done, allow to cool. Store in freezer for 10-25 years.

Serves no one

What Will You Sacrifice to Pursue Your Mission?

While I believe that the pursuit of your mission will ultimately give you a greater sense of purpose, a renewed perspective on life, and a sense of fulfillment unmatched by false success alone, I also know that you will have to make sacrifices in order to surrender to your mission. Since I have personally made a jailbreak from the prison of success, I thought I would share some of the things that were difficult for me and some of the things that I thought would be difficult, but were not.

Simple Sacrifices

Of everything that I sacrificed when I broke free of false success, probably the easiest was money. I have always been thrifty (okay, I'm a tightwad) and I had built up my savings and made wise investments to make the transition a little bit easier, but there were a few unforeseen expenses that thumped me in the back of the head as well.

I was progressively moving higher up the ladder and was in the habit of relocating with my company once about every two years. Blinded by false success, I treated each of my relocations as a celebration of my continual conquest as I ascended the aforementioned ladder. My job was demanding, stressful, and sometimes very frustrating but my reward was a generous income and very good benefits. I thought I owed it to my family and myself to buy bigger, more expensive homes with each move to offset the difficulties of my job and to make a public profession of my success. If you have been through the relocation process with large companies, you know that this is generally a low-risk endeavor because the company will pay closing costs when you sell your home and real estate values tend to climb. In some cases, they will even buy your old house from you if it does not sell within a certain timeframe.

If you decide to leave the company, however, you are on your own. This is precisely what happened to us. In the three relocations that I had made with my company prior to this move, all three houses sold in a grand total of one week! Because of this, I never had to use the buyout clause and had a very warped sense of how easy it was to sell a home. When I decided to leave my job, we purchased our new home while our old one was still on the market thinking that we would just have to carry a double mortgage for a month or two. This was during 2006, when the residential real estate market really started to cool off. Furthermore, the house that we were trying to sell was in a rural area in Nebraska—not exactly a hotspot for growth. On top of this, a large employer in the area shut its doors, causing the housing demand to weaken even more. To make matters worse, we got a letter from our mortgage company one month after we moved informing us that the real estate taxes used for our escrow estimate was incorrect and that our monthly mortgage payment was going to increase by another two hundred fifty dollars per month!

Talk about frustrating! I gave up a high-paying job to try to do something on my own and was paying two mortgages—one of which was already the biggest mortgage we ever had before going up another two hundred fifty dollars for a house that we couldn't even see, let alone live in because it was twelve hundred miles away. For the first time in my life, I had to make a budget and monitor it closely to make sure we kept our spending in check. Fourteen months later, we sold our old house for substantially less than we had originally paid for it.

I am telling you this story not to prepare you for financial hardships and warn you of the associated sacrifices, but to illustrate something that I learned during those lean times. Despite the difficulty of having two mortgages, a reduced income, and putting many of our wants on hold, my wife and I never had any regrets about my decision to leave my success behind. It was difficult, frustrating, and little bit scary, but it was also a relief to have escaped the prison of success. We never lacked anything that we needed, we were reassured of the support and love of our families, and we were no less happy than when we were comfortably stashing away savings. In many ways, we were happier. It is very liberating to know from firsthand experience that your financial situation does not dictate your happiness.

At some point, you have heard the phrase, "You don't know what you've got 'til it's gone." Maybe you heard this after ending a relationship, losing a loved one, or from the mullet-clad wisdom of Cinderella (the 80's band, not the Disney character). This adage may be true for relationships and our basic needs, but I don't think it holds up when it comes to material possessions and false success. In fact, for these things I think it would be more appropriate to say, "You don't know how little you need them, 'til they're gone."

If you need further proof, just look at the people who are wildly successful financially. For the most part, these people focus on how to earn additional money (climbing up the corporate ladder), how to turn the money they already have into more money (investments), and how to protect the money they have made (tax evasion). No matter how much they have, it is never enough and it will never give them a sense of significance. That is one of the interesting dynamics when it comes to wealth—the more you have of it, the more you feel that you need it.

Don't get me wrong, part of your responsibility as an adult is to make financial plans to provide for your family. This includes earning money and investing it wisely. However, the procurement and growth of money should not be your greatest motivator. If it is, you are placing your hopes in an existence devoid of true fulfillment and a future of ever-increasing need. The only way to get a grip on this is to experience it yourself. Having experienced it, I can tell you that the sacrifice of wealth is a simple one to make when faced with the opportunity to pursue your passions.

Difficult Sacrifices

While giving up my income was not as hard as I expected, other sacrifices proved to be more difficult. These sacrifices primarily centered on my ego and included the following: the loss of responsibility, the loss of authoritative presence, and the loss of my professional identity. These aspects of my job gave me a sense of importance. They made me feel needed; so when I decided to leave my job, it only follows that I felt less needed.

In terms of responsibility, I was once responsible for all manufacturing operations in a multimillion dollar operation with several hundred employees that ran twenty-four hours a day, seven days a week. There were constant problems to deal with, calls at all hours of the night (and weekends, and holidays, and vacations…), and I felt like I could never let down my guard because as soon a one problem was resolved, a new one took its place. Despite all of the inherent stress that comes along with responsibility, we have a desire (particularly men) to be an essential need to others. We sometimes feel validated in the moments of crisis. By removing ourselves from the environments that give birth to those crises, we risk losing our identity.

This feeling of lost identity goes back to our habit of categorizing our existence according to our careers. Because we turn away from our passions and refuse to become truly alive by seeking to fulfill our mission, we resort to what we feel is the next best thing—success. Typically, this is the world's view of success that we achieve through our careers. Our careers become a surrogate for our personal mission and we mysteriously have difficulty leaving a career that will never offer us true success, fulfillment, or significance because we rely on it for our identity and sense of purpose. We do this oblivious to the fact that because we refuse to follow our passions, the identity and sense of purpose created by our careers is not our true selves. This results in a tension that is present in the lives of multitudes of successful professionals. The identity that they have created through their careers has the outward appearance of success and happiness, but inwardly, they experience severe conflict.

When viewed in this manner, it would seem that shifting our focus from a career based on false success to the pursuit of our mission would be a great relief and we could do so with no regrets. Well, it's not that easy. For me, I did feel relieved to get out of the daily grind and away from the frustrations of my old career. On the other hand, there was a sense of loss from the amount of responsibility that I had freely relinquished. Like many of you, I had been dead to my passions for so long I no longer believed it would be prudent to follow them. Instead, I focused my time and energy on being successful on other people's terms. The more I invested in this identity, the more difficult it became for me to turn away from it.

I am telling you this because I feel that it is important for you to understand the importance of completely surrendering to your mission. If you do not take the time to understand your purpose and your passions or if you only pursue them with a half-hearted effort, the fulfillment that you receive from the pursuit of your passions will not outweigh the remorse that you will feel from giving up the identity that you have worked so hard to create. True, that old identity may not be the real you, but if you are not fully committed to your mission and capitalizing on your skills and talents, then your new pursuit will not be the real you either. You will again fall into the pursuit of false success—you will simply be taking a different path to get there.

The key point here is that if you intend to escape from the imprisonment of false success, you must be prepared to give up the psychological crutches it provides. You will need to have faith in the fact that the significance of your mission will outweigh the comfort of your successful identity. You will have to believe that the outcome of your mission will be more compelling and fulfilling than the positional authority of your career. Ultimately, you must know that the responsibility you bear in utilizing your specific gifts to fulfill your own unique mission is far greater than the generic responsibility bestowed upon you as a cog in the great machine of false success.

What Sacrifices Are You Not Willing To Make?

In addition to coming to terms with the sacrifices you may need to make along your journey, you need to know which sacrifices you should not make. These will be unique to each individual, but we all have areas in our lives we should never compromise even if this means that it will make the pursuit of our mission more difficult. Some of these areas include:

- Religious beliefs
- Prioritizing our family before our careers
- Ethics/morals
- Environmental stewardship
- Social responsibilities
- Seeking/promoting the truth
- Welfare of others

If you take the leap to pursue your passions, you will no longer be limited to the world of superficial false success. Your victories will not measured by the size of your paycheck or your assent up the corporate ladder. You will have the opportunity to experience the fulfillment of true success and you will have a much stronger desire meet your goals because they will be in alignment with your personal mission. This powerful and liberating aspect is deeply gratifying, but it also bears significant responsibility. The pursuit of your mission must not come at the expense of those areas in your life that you refuse to sacrifice. It may be more difficult to maintain integrity as you pursue your mission because you will be so committed to it and passionate about it.

Nobody Said this Would be Easy

Like many of you, I daydreamed about striking out on my own and pursuing my passions. I had come to terms with the notion that I would be taking a serious pay cut, at least initially. I accepted that many people would not understand my decision and possibly even view me as a quitter. I realized that I would be relinquishing the positional authority that I had worked so hard to acquire. Yet for several years, I could not bring myself to take that initial step of leaving my job and the false success that it offered. Like many of my coworkers, I lacked the courage to follow through on my dreams.

We have become a society of cowards. We like to talk about how great life would be if only we go back to school to get a degree in an area that interests us; if only we could move to a particular location; or if only we could find fulfillment by pursuing a meaningful mission ... but that's where it ends—with talk. We have become so theoretical and philosophical about the way things *could* be that we waste our time creating a perfect existence in our minds without taking the necessary action of implementing practical measures right now.

It seems that we sometimes like our dreams to remain dreams. That way, they are untainted by the sweat, grime, and ugliness that is often necessary to make dreams come true. In this same twisted manner, we also seem to have an affinity for those things that bring us heartache in our daily routines. It is as if we fear that the removal of our sources of heartache would require us to live our lives with a full heart. A full heart is not what most of us signed up for when we started our careers. Even the notion of a full heart implies a softness that runs contrary to the vast majority or our society's perception of success. We think that in order to achieve profound success, you must be a sleep-deprived, stoic workaholic who puts their careers before their families and their own personal wellbeing in order keep climbing the ladder. Ultimately, the only thing with which false success fills our hearts is the fatty deposits that result from too much stress and cholesterol.

Despite the frustration, emptiness, and unbalance caused by false success, very few of us actually let go of it. We may not like the life we are living, but at least it is familiar to us. How pathetic is that? We may complain about our careers, bosses, coworkers, or employers but ultimately, seeking our fulfillment is our own responsibility. If you feel that your search for significance is taking you somewhere else, but you refuse to go, then you are a coward who will continue to have an empty heart. No matter what you try to do to fill it up, whether it be material possessions, job titles, ever-increasing responsibility, or even charitable works, the emptiness will remain until you completely surrender to your mission. This is why bravery is so important. From an outsider's perspective, a miserable person with false success may appear to be better off than a financially struggling person who has surrendered to their mission. In reality, the biggest difference between these two people is not their bank accounts. The biggest difference between these two people is in their hearts. The one dedicated to their mission experiences a fulfillment the likes of which the other will never know. Unfortunately, few actually experience this feeling because most of us refuse to give up the false success we have attained.

Epilogue

I wish you the best on your journey and I hope this book made you think about who you are, what motivates you, and how you can pursue your passions. By writing this, I didn't set out to impress anyone with my literary talents (however little I may possess). In fact, I know that by letting others read the pages of this book, I am setting myself up for judgment and criticism. I'm fine with that because I feel that one of my missions is to tell my story. As I said, following your mission takes courage, humility, and the willingness to step outside your area of expertise. For a person trained in engineering with no literary background, writing this book certainly required all of these things of me. Nevertheless, I will not allow my efforts in writing this book to be marginalized by the very concepts that the book was meant to expose. I feel deeply that people need to hear my story because they struggle with the same issues and if just one person chooses to seek a life of significance over a life of success after reading this, then the whole experience has been worth the effort.

Throughout this book, I came back to the thought that we have an emptiness within us that we try to fill with success. As a Christian, I believe that this emptiness is ultimately a result of our separation from God due to sin (see the part about Adam and Eve) and the only way that we can be restored to Him is through Jesus Christ. If you are not a Christian, I want you to consider your life and what it is missing. If you are a Christian, but still feel emptiness, I challenge you to stop living as if you can create purpose from your effort and start aligning your efforts with your mission.

About the Author

Jason Barr was born and raised in the small town of Medina, Tennessee. He graduated from Tennessee Technological University in Cookeville, Tennessee with a degree in mechanical engineering. After graduating from college, Jason moved to Ohio, Indiana, Florida, New York, and Nebraska seeking success with numerous corporate transfers and promotions.

A discontentment with the corporate lifestyle, a series of nationally publicized corporate scandals, the birth of his first daughter, and the death of a family member led Jason to leave his corporate career. No longer chasing success, Jason lives in a suburb of northeast Atlanta with his wife, Sara, and two daughters, Olivia and Amelia, where he enjoys spending time with his family, reading, hiking, and is active in his local church, New Bethany Baptist Church.

In pursuit of his mission, Jason wrote this book, created a blog (http://significantblog.wordpress.com), travels to Eastern Europe to teach English, and is available for speaking engagements. Jason freely admits that he is still a work in progress, and is confident that if he can give up the quest for false success, so can you.

Printed in the United States
132870LV00005B/151/P